THE BALANCE OF THE CROSS IS ALWAYS A PLUS

THE BALANCE OF THE CROSS IS ALWAYS A PLUS

Unique Learning Through Creative Communication

JIM ELARDE

The Balance of the Cross is Always a Plus by James Elarde

ISBN: 978-1-59755-722-1

Published by: ADVANTAGE BOOKS™, Longwood, Florida, USA
www.advbookstore.com

Library of Congress Catalog Number: 2023935383

Name: Elarde, James, Author
Title: ***The Balance of the Cross is Always a Plus***
Advantage Books, 2022
Identifiers: ISBN Paperback: 9781597557221, eBook: 9781597557375
Subject: Christian Life: Inspirational

First Printing: March 2023
23 24 25 26 27 28 10 9 8 7 6 5 4

Table of Contents

INTRODUCTION **9**

SECTION ONE: THE PLUS WORDS AND THE BALANCE OF THE CROSS **11**

PULLING THE CROSS OUT OF BALANCE **13**

KEEPING THE SCRIPTURE IN BALANCE **14**

WITH A CORRECT VIEW OF SIN **14**

NINE PLACES WHERE CHRISTIANS MIGHT BE OUT OF BALANCE IN THEIR WALK! **17**

- SERVANTS OF GOD OUR NEW IDENTITY! 17
- UNITY, DIVERSITY AND TOTAL ACCEPTANCE 17
- LOOKING FOR EACH OTHER-GOD AND US! 18
- BOND SERVANTS FIRST WITH DESIGNATED GIFTS TO EMPLOY 19
- VERTICAL AND HORIZONTAL RELATIONSHIP! 20
- ALL THINGS WORK FOR GOOD WITH RECIPROCAL LOVE TO GOD! 20
- CORRECT QUALIFICATIONS- IF YOU DO WHAT I COMMAND! 21
- VICTORY WITH LOVE OVER SUFFERING! NO AVOIDANCE! 21
- THE PERIL OF MONEY 23

REPENTANCE IS A GIFT BY OPTION ONLY! **26**

MOVING AT GODS PACE-- IN THE LORD! **28**

UNDERSTANDING FROM GOD'S PERSPECTIVE **30**

LOVE AND GOOD DEEDS ALWAYS! - MIRACLES ON OCCASION - **33**

CHANGES IN TECHNOLOGY AND HOW - IT IS AFFECTING THE CHURCH **35**

THE HEAD AND THE HEART - SHOULD NEVER WORK APART! **37**

MERCY AND GRACE IS A - TWO FOLD HELP PACKAGE **40**

GOD'S ELECTION FOR ALL TO BE SAVED! **43**

FIGHTING TEMPTATION GOD'S WAY **47**

OVERLOOK THE TRANSGRESSIONS - OF OTHERS IN TWO WAYS **50**

BE—COME > THE RIGHTEOUSNESS - OF GOD IN CHRIST 53

FORGIVENESS AND RECONCILIATION - WE DO BOTH 56

FALLEN CREATURES AND RESPONSIBLE PERSONS CRY FOR MERCY! 59

GOD'S VERY BIG PART SHOWS US - THE EXTENT OF HIS LOVING HEART! 62

PART TWO OF GOD'S VERY BIG HEART! 67

A CLEAR LOOK AT WHAT HARDENS A PERSON'S HEART 70

MERCY AND GRACE +JUSTICE AND RIGHTEOUSNESS 72

THE POWER OF GOD'S HOLINESS - UNIQUE AND ONE OF A KIND! 75

THE DEEPEST INTIMACY WITH GOD! 77

WISDOM IS MUCH MORE THAN MAKING WISE CHOICES 82

SECTION TWO: GOD'S CREATIVE COMMUNICATION 85

THE GREAT BREAKER AND TRAINER! 87

THE TREES OF THE FIELD WILL CLAP THEIR HANDS 98

PART C: SURVEY TIME FROM CHRIST THE VINE! 105

IT'S NOT ME IT'S MR. DUNAMIS! 108

THE PRELIMINARY HEARING OF FAITH MEMBERS OF THE HIGHEST COURT! 115

THE HARE AND THE TORTOISE 121

FROM THE ROAD WITH EVIL TO THE EXPRESSWAY TO HEAVEN 127

HYBRIDS ON THE HIGHWAY TO HEAVEN! 127

CAPTAIN GOD WANTS FIRST MATES TO HANDLE HIS FISHING BUSINESS! 135

SUCCESS IN THE HIGHEST WAY POSSIBLE! 143

THE BEST IS FOR LAST WHEN THE WORLD'S IN YOUR PAST! 147

THE HOST, THE BAKER, THE GRILL MAN AND THE WAITER! 152

TWO FLIES ON A CLEAR CLEAN WINDOW---A TURN AROUND EVENT! 156

A CHRISTMAS MESSAGE FOR THE PRESENT TIME! 159

HUMILITY FIRST FOR GOD TO MEET THIRST! 161

GENTLENESS IS THE GLOVE OF LOVE FOR THE HUMBLE HAND! 167

GODS FELLOWSHIP IN HIMSELF - WHERE PERFECT LOVE STARTS! 175

A SUITABLE HELPER 178

IS VARIETY THE SPICE OF LIFE? 179

HOW A MAN SHOULD LOVE A WOMAN GOD'S WAY! 180

THERE IS NO DOOR IN WHICH TEARS DO NOT PASS WITH GRIEF OR JOY 185

CRUCIFIED WITH CHRIST AND RAISED TO GLORY! 188

SECTION THREE: FINE DIVINE RHYME TIME 192

The Wilderness the Wilderness 192
Hands of Hope the Extension of God's Kindness! 193
Overflow Should Always Go! 194
Lord Touch us again and again and again! 195
Stop Climbing the Steps of the Crowded Ladder 196
Mr. In and Out? Or Mr. Steadfast? 197
Why Should We Pray? 198
Me! Me! Me!—How Self-Centered can Me Be? 200
Mercy and Grace God's Mercy and Grace 201
Obedience is a Humble Affair! 202
Get off Your Lofty Pedestal 202
Walk and Talk the Gospel 203
Face to Face in Fellowship Gods with me Gods here! 204
Move in Faith and Walk in Love 205
Sought--Brought---Bought---Preach---Teach---Keep! 206
God's Way not my way! Sing It! 207
The Holy Spirit is the Real Mr. Clean! Sing It! 208

Introduction

The purpose of this book is for Christians to see and learn a balance of freedom in their walk with God and to know Jesus better by standing under Him as our Lord and Savior. We can learn how to reciprocate love back to God out of humility, honor, and gratitude for who He is and all He has done for those in Christ. This seems to be a common purpose for true Christianity and should be above any other purpose in life. It is the only purpose that will move from this fallen earth into eternity. God is the truth and the essence of life. All of life starts with God and never ends with God. He is the One and only God, and He has given us His Son and His Spirit to verify the facts. He has left us with the book of love and the instruction book of life. We can know a balanced life with a balanced interpretation of how to succeed by looking at the Word of the Cross as a big plus sign. It will always add to our life the truth of God, the way of Jesus, and the reason we live and move and have our being. The Word of the Cross is a story above and beyond all stories that are birthed as an offspring to it. Every person's story is a small extension from the eternal story that God was and is, and will always be. He came to earth in Christ to rescue us with His love and wants to reconcile us to Himself so that we can live forever with Him for His good pleasure. It is wise to believe the Bible as the absolute truth in all of its writing and know where a small portion of it is written in general truths. The sum of all scripture can bring the only accurate interpretations from the inspired Word, which was written by the Holy Spirit through the men He moved and breathed His message to. Anyone who sits at the feet of Jesus Christ in solitude before they start another day in this temporary world will experience the greatest three eternal persons of the universe and the One and only God; The essence of life, light, love, and wisdom. I am so glad God is the (I Am that I Am!) This is where we must start, and He is where life will never end! With all humility, honor, and gratitude to God, and by His Mercy, Grace, and privilege of knowing God in Christ, He has qualified me to share in His Glorious Life by His Great Kindness and Love! Jim Elarde, Bond Servant of God + Minister of Creative Communication in God's Word.

Section One

The Plus Words and The Balance of the Cross

As Christians, we must focus on the Word of the Cross and the necessity to handle the word correctly and in balance from the sum of all Scripture. We don't focus on parts of the Scripture but all of the word to help us come to a balanced interpretation. We must recognize all the plus words in the text of the book of life. I hope to present you with several illustrations on how to live in balance which will bring freedom to us in Christ. A plus word will be a conjunction in a sentence to combine the whole unit of thought and make us realize we can't be extreme toward one part of the text and neglect another part of what it is saying. By doing that, the word of the cross would be acted on in a way that pulls it out of balance and causes us to deviate from the truth we need to live with. Some of the common plus words translated into English are used often, but many people fail to realize how important they are in the structure of each sentence. Here are some common plus words we all know and read to join the topic being discussed. I will list them, and you will eventually see that these words bring us toward the balance of interpretation in how the Scripture should be applied. Here is the most common one. The word and is so important because of its inclusiveness to balance what is being said. Another word is but. Then we have two words used together, according to, then if, also, yet, with, and more words that act as important conjunctions. Then is one I just used two times. In Scripture, each word connects the two sides of what is being said in the verses or units of thought from God's Word. + Do you notice that this plus sign looks the same as a cross someone might put around their neck? There could not be a stronger connection because living by the Word of the Cross is always going to ADD to a person's life! Do you see how it represents balance just by looking at it? The vertical and horizontal positions are joined at 90-degree angles. The vertical is perfectly straight up, and the horizontal is straight across. Picture a circus performer walking the high wire. What is he holding to keep his balance? A pole with both arms. He has to stand perfectly straight in a vertical position, and the pole has to be straight across his body in a horizontal position. If he performs without a pole, he puts his arms straight out in a horizontal way, and his body stands in a vertical position and he forms the sign of the cross with his body to stay balanced. We know as Christians that the Cross is also the anchor for our soul. Without the death and resurrection of Jesus, there is no forgiveness of sins and eternal life. The Cross always has two sides that keep it standing in a perfect balance. One side would tell us Mercy and Grace is for us, and the other side would say wrath, righteousness, and justice must be present. Both sides are always in the heart and mind of God.

Pulling the Cross out of Balance

We all need a balanced life in many ways. We need to avoid extremes that pull us out of balance and include things that can keep us in balance. Here are two verses that make this easy to understand. Ecclesiastes 4:5-6 says-The fool folds his hands and consumes his own flesh. One hand full of rest is better than two fists full of labor and striving after the wind. These two statements tell us we have to live between them to keep a balanced life. In the first one, the fool pulls the cross down on the left side. The man refuses to work and is disobedient and out of balance with the mandate of God's word that we all do work with diligence. In the second part, the man pulls the cross down to the right side. He takes no time to rest, indicating greed with his fists clenched tightly, grabbing all he can get from working too much and neglecting rest and perhaps his family also. He is striving after the wind, for the love of money will be sowing to the wind. No work or too much work is pulling the cross out of balance. A handful of each brings balance to our lives.

This is what we need >>>> + Not this >>>> X

Keeping the Scripture in Balance with a correct view of Sin

Romans 6:1-2 speaks balance to us in a very big way! Are we to continue in sin so grace may increase? God forbid, or may it never be! <These are all the + words).

How can we who died to sin still live in it? John 8:11 is the perfect verse on balance. Jesus says to the woman caught in adultery, "I do not condemn you (go and + words) sin no more." One side of the cross is I do not condemn you! We love this side. The plus words, (go, and +) or (from now on +) sin no more. We may not be in love with this side yet! Titus 2: 11-12 are very good verses to live life in balance by the word of the cross. For the grace of God has appeared, bringing salvation to all men (instructing us to + words) deny ungodliness and worldly desires and to live sensibly, righteously, and godly in this present age. Here are some scriptures that Christians find comfort in, but they may be out of balance with the correct interpretation.

Isiah 43:25, I am the one who wipes out your transgressions for My own sake, and I will not remember your sins.

Micah 7:19, God will again have compassion on us; He will tread our iniquities underfoot. Lord, you will cast all their sins into the depths of the sea.

Psalm 103:12, As far as the east is from the west, So far God has removed our transgressions from us.

Romans 4:8-Blessed is the man whose sin the Lord will not take into account.

John 1:29, Behold the Lamb of God who takes away the sin of the world! All of these are very comforting to read. Here comes the balance of scripture verses so we can look at sin correctly.

Proverbs 15:3, the eyes of the Lord are in every place watching both the evil and the good.

Hosea 7:-2 And they do not consider in their hearts that I remember all their wickedness. Now their deeds are all around them: They are before My face.

Hosea 13:12-The iniquity of Ephraim is bound up; His sin is stored up.

Eccl. 8:11- Because the sentence against an evil deed is not executed quickly, the hearts of many men take sin too lightly and are given fully to do evil. Combine this with Colossians 3:25- For he who does wrong will receive the consequences of the wrong he has done without partiality.

1st John 3-9 says, (No one who is born of God practices sin, because God's seed abides in him, and he cannot sin, because he is born of God.)

How should we look at sin and be balanced in our view of how we live? Draw a cross for yourself and put these scriptures on the corresponding sides. Draw a line from the verses on both sides from the horizontal part toward the ground and anchor it to the ground.

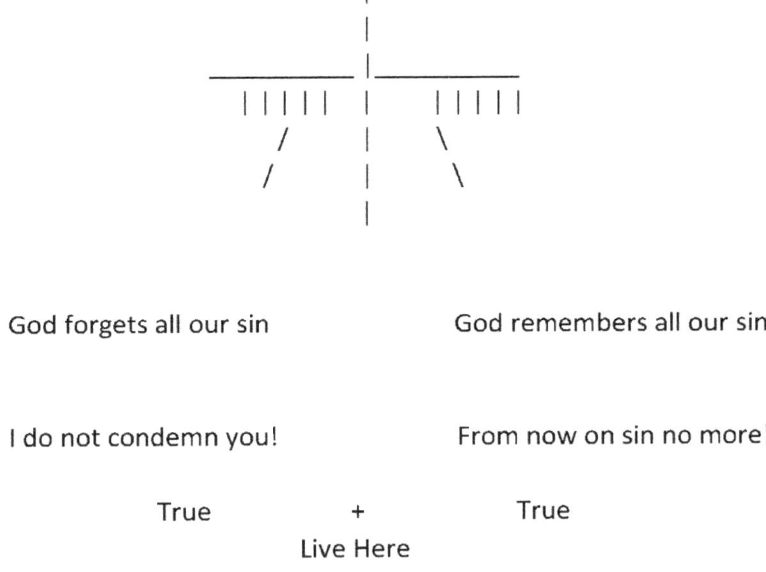

If you only have the scriptures on one side and neglect the scriptures on the other side, you will be pulling the word of the cross out of balance.

It will look like this

>>>>>> X <<<<<<

When it looks like an (X), it means to cross it out. It is not working! Isn't it interesting we cross wrong answers out with an X and not a balanced-looking cross? A teacher will say; You can cross out that answer. It is wrong. Because the answer is incorrect, it is out of balance with the truth. Understand God does not stop remembering sins. For the believer, He will no longer hold them against us or throw them in our face like the devil does, wanting us to feel condemned. Our account is clean from a legal perspective. From a moral one, we are hindering our walk with God by sins we refuse to repent of. (From now on) or (Go and sin no more) are words we need to think deeper about and start acting upon! If we do sin, we have an advocate in Jesus Christ, the righteous one! But, there will still be very unpleasant consequences if we get caught in continual sins.

Nine places where Christians might be out of Balance in their walk!

Servants of God Our New Identity!

Romans 6:18 tells us after being freed from sin, we became slaves of righteousness. We need to look at the word (became). It is a past tense word telling us slaves or servants of righteousness is not to be looked at as what we do but as who we are in Christ. The church often asks for people to volunteer to help with something that lines up with the word of God. After they hear this, many Christians focus on what is to be done and not who they became in Christ. This gets a lesser response from Christians. If we realized we were sentenced to be God's servant when He freed us from sin, we would realize we must serve out of obedience instead of the preference to comply or not comply as a volunteer. The world can get volunteers to promote a common grace act that helps, and it's okay. But God has servants or slaves of righteousness. Here is what makes the motive correct for the serving act; God said to do as he did! Jesus went from suffering servant to glorified servant forever! The best the world gets is a good works trip. With us, it should be whatever He says in His word, DO IT! (John 2:5) or stop doing what is wrong!

Unity, Diversity and Total Acceptance

We need to see this in the body of Christ; The unity we must have and the acceptance of diversity we function in. All the body parts work together and each part has a different function. We are different personalities unified in love and accepted in all our differences. By not comparing ourselves to one another in a childish way, we allow everyone to function. God has given all of us One Spirit to guide and control. No one should be quick to judge a brother or sister or exalt themselves above another person. With humility first, God will meet thirst. We are to know our spiritual gifts and use them accordingly. Proper placement is very important, and one does not earn their position in function. The Holy Spirit has given to each as He has determined. (1st Corinthians 12:11). God brings us up when we cooperate with Him, and we do not earn or work our way up. The world climbs up the crowded ladder. We are raised up with reward and honor from God. A reward is not earned like a wage is. Wages are expected, but rewards should not be expected. Grace is a gift and our proper functions are from our giftedness. If someone misses a church meeting on occasion, don't take a tally or be quick to say where were you last week? It takes more than a week or two for a person to miss someone they need to spend much time to get to know. They could be leading someone to God or helping someone by being the church in action, meeting a pressing need. Every day Christians have multiple options. Allow people to make choices and pray they serve God wherever they are at any time. Watch out for spiritual pride. Love and pray for all people without ceasing. Unity is one side of the cross, and diversity is the other side. We must be in balance for God in One Essence is three in Personhood. He is unified and He is diverse. He is fully present everywhere all the time. We can only be in one place at a time. Receive the wisdom to allow freedom of choice to all and pray we all make godly choices.

Looking for each other-God and Us!

Does God really do all of the choosing of those who come into His loving Mercy and Grace? Yes, because the chosen ones said yes to his offer by their free will choice. There are Bible verses where God tells us to seek His Face and search for Him so He can be found by us. And there are verses where God seeks to save us and searches for us to be His children. The Bible says we should be looking for each other. Look for God and know He is looking for you also. There are two sides to the search. Luke 19:10, for the Son of man has come to seek and save that which was lost. John 4:23B, those who worship in spirit and truth the Father seeks to be His worshipers. John 15:16-You did not choose me, but I chose you and appointed you to bear fruit that will remain. 2nd Chron. 16:9, the eyes of the Lord move to and fro throughout the earth that He may support those whose heart is completely His. Revelation 3:20, Behold, I stand at the door and knock; if anyone hears my voice and opens the door, I will come in to him and will dine with him, and he with Me. The other side of the cross, where we should seek God, has many verses. Because we forget God, He has told us repeatedly in His word to remember the Lord our God and seek Him while He may be found. Jer.29:13 says- You will seek Me and find Me when you search for Me with all your heart. Isiah 55:6, Seek the Lord while He may be found; Call upon Him while He is near. Psalm 27:8, When You said, Seek My face, my heart said to You, Your face, O Lord, I shall seek. Zep.2:3, Seek the Lord, All you humble of the earth who have carried out His ordinances; Seek righteousness, seek humility. Acts 17:26-27, and He (God) made from one man every nation of mankind to live on all the face of the earth. He determined their appointed times and boundaries of their habitation that they should seek God if perhaps they might grope for Him and find Him, though He is not far from each one of us. To find God implies reconciliation to Christ through redemption and accepting His physical and spiritual death in our place so He can bring us through our first death into

His resurrection life forever. I would recommend that all people stop playing hide and seek with God. We are the ones that hide, and it would be much better to seek Him. He is not hiding from us. He does not want to be the one doing all the seeking. He came in Jesus to seek and save us once and for all. He has left the truth with us. His witness is everywhere, and the proof has been established. Stop hiding and let His love remove your pride. He is present everywhere, longing to love you. Reach out and take hold of His great salvation. In Luke 19:1-10 Jesus looks up and sees Zaccheus has climbed a tree to meet Him. Jesus enjoys his determined effort and calls him out of the tree. Zaccheus, come down. I must stay at your house today. I would like to have a meal with you. Quickly he obeys because He is not one who hides. For Jesus is seeking to save, and Zaccheus is looking for Him and excited to meet God in all His glory in Christ. They have a meal together, and Zaccheus repents of his sin. Salvation has come to the house of Zaccheus. An intimate search is over for both sides, and life has been explained! Looking for each other will result in reconciliation with God when we seek Him wholeheartedly. Would you climb a tree to meet Jesus?

Bond Servants first with designated gifts to employ

We never separate our gifts and talents from God with the fact that we have become His servants. God is the complete ruler of our heart and life. When you read all the salutations that begin many books of the New Testament, you can see the opening greetings from each writer. They say things like Paul, a bondservant of God called as an Apostle of Jesus Christ. This is the cross. One side is who Paul has become in Christ, a bondservant. The other side is his purpose of function. He is the Apostle and missionary. He is not the Apostle without being the slave and servant of righteousness by God's doing!

Romans 6:18 and 1 Corinthians 1:30. This will help us when we employ our gifts from God to do them in humility and love and never in pride. We bear fruit from serving with love and good deeds, and we have the delegated power to change other people's lives. There's the act of love and an intimate service to others plus+ the resurrection power of God being displayed through us. The cross is always a plus+, and it adds the life of God to others. The heart of humility and service is where God can demonstrate His power through us. As a Christian, it will always be this way and there is no room for the pride of the flesh at any time. Knowing God and making Him known to others is a great privilege. Interpret what the salutations are saying and recognize and remember that only bond servants do the work of God for His glory. It is good to adopt this statement that I have always kept for myself. Lord, it is such a privilege and pleasure to watch you work! He will get all the glory, and we will see to it!

Vertical and Horizontal Relationship!

Reconciliation has priority over religion. Reconciliation to Christ gives us the vertical part of Solitude with God and the horizontal part of bringing God's presence to others. The practice of solitude is what Jesus always did before He ministered most effectively to others. He prayed in solitude with the Father for hours. Then, He spent long days bringing the gospel to all people. With us, the only difference is we pray and study the word of God diligently so we know the truth, for we are all people who need God. Jesus is the truth the Bible is written about. He is the living word of the living God. We need both sides to be in balance and they must not be neglected. We will not succeed without spending time alone with God and + doing the word of God to and for others. Religion will fail, but love and good deeds from intimate reconciliation and fellowship with God will not fail. His word being lived through us will not return empty, but it will accomplish all He sent it to accomplish. The cross is always adding vertical and horizontal relationships that put God first to fill everyone's thirst!

All things work for good with reciprocal love to God!

Romans 8:28 is quoted by many when they are going through very tough circumstances. The first side of the verse is: And we know that God causes all things to work together for good. Then we have the connecting words, which are the (plus + words), to those who love God, and the last part of the verse, to those who are called according to His purpose. God makes it clear when Jesus speaks to the disciples in John 14:15. If you love Me, you will keep My commandments. We love Him by obeying His word. Now, let's look at those who are called according to His purpose. According to means, in keeping with, as determined by, on the authority of–Keeping with God's plan and purpose, as determined by God's plan and purpose, on the authority of God's commands for us. There must be an effort of submission and obedience to the degree that we reciprocate love back to God because He loved us first. We love because He first loved us. (1st John 4:19) Obedience is the only true gage to loving God. It is always reciprocal, but how can one expect things to turn out good if they are disobedient and neglect God and His purpose? They may be living for their selfish purposes. He does not demand perfection from us, and He knows our flesh is weak. We know we can't be perfect but suppose the tough things you are going through are a result of your continuous sins. You may not be confessing them or repenting from them. Would you still expect God to turn your situation around and neglect the discipline you need out of His Holy love for you? Examine your life and see how it will turn out good after you listen and repent. If a person sins against you and you are suffering for it, you can know God will work it out for good, but you will still have to respond correctly and give it to God to handle. You can't allow bitterness, and we are told to forgive. We are not to retaliate or take vengeance into our own hands. It comes down to entrusting yourself to your loving God and watching Him work it out for good.

Correct Qualifications- if you do what I command!

John 15:14 Jesus says- You are My friends if you do what I command you. The first side is you are My friends. The plus word here is the biggest little word in the dictionary (IF). The other side of the IF word is, you do what I command. Many Christians are bringing Jesus down to their level as a friend while they are living in disobedience. Oh, Jesus is my best friend! Are you obeying His commands? How much love are you reciprocating for the love He has given you? You could be saying He is your best friend when you are not qualifying to be a friend to Him. Take heed to what He said; I call you friends +if+ you do what I command you. This is a balance we need to have and realize. You are not acting like God's friend when you are living in disobedience. You are a son or daughter forever when you are born again with the Holy Spirit's regeneration. But discipline is coming when you are not acting like one God wants to call His friend. We never bring Jesus down to our level. We long for His fellowship and humble ourselves before Him, bowing to His commands and learning obedience.

Victory with Love over suffering! No Avoidance!

The suffering in this world always puts us in a position where we long for comfort. We will look closely and see how Christians are out of balance when they always desire to be comfortable. In 2nd Corinthians 1: 3-7, God is described as the God of all comfort. It is written in regard to the sufferings we go through as Christians, and it does not refer to being comfortable by never going through affliction. If God gave us all a rose garden, there would be thorns to cause pain as long as we are in this world. Jesus had a crown of thorns before His crown of glory! Christians are not called to a life of comfort and ease. Real Christians are persecuted and abused at times. If a Christian is effective in his call from

God he will experience rejection and trouble from unbelievers. New Christians seem to get the playpen and nursery time; after they start to grow, it can be very difficult to avoid conflicts. God will comfort us so we can minister to others with the same comfort we received. Our experience and testimony helps others get through their suffering. (2nd Cor. 1)

Acts 8:1-4 says great persecution came against the church, and many Christians were persecuted. This was written following the stoning of Stephen in the 7th chapter. He died, giving glory to God and asking God to forgive the evildoers who stoned him. Here are the verses on one side of the cross that we can't avoid.

Philippians 3:10-11 says, we will share in the sufferings of Christ.

1st Peter 4:13 says all the sufferings we go through because we are in Christ should give us a reason to rejoice, for we will share in His glory when He returns. 1st Corinthians 16:9, Paul says, for a wide door for effective service has opened to me, and there are many adversaries.

2nd Timothy 3:11-12 says all who desire to live godly in Christ Jesus will be persecuted. The other side of the cross on suffering is that glory is coming and can't be compared to the suffering.

Romans 8:18 says the sufferings of this present time can't be compared to the glory that is to be revealed to us.

2nd Corinthians 4:17 says it is momentary light affliction producing an eternal weight of glory far beyond all comparison.

We do not love pain and embrace the pain itself, but we embrace the will of God. Jesus wanted to escape from Gethsemane and shun the cross as a man would. He went to the cross as an obedient Son and embraced the Father's will. Showing all the love and courage possible, He conquered death and completed the plan of eternal life for all who will follow Him and trust Him with their life. We must endure suffering with joy, knowing we have our wonderful, indescribable future and inheritance with Christ from God.

James 1:2-4 says Consider it all joy when you encounter various trials and the testing of your faith that produces endurance. Endurance or perseverance makes us complete in our character. It helps us accept the whole word of God and the fellowship of Jesus' suffering. We know we will receive the promise of eternal life as we trust in God to sanctify us and conform us to the image of Jesus. Conformed to His death, we will be conformed to His body of glory! (Philippians 3:20-21.)

1st Peter 5:10 says that after you have suffered for a little while, the God of all grace who called you to His eternal glory in Christ will perfect, confirm, strengthen and establish you. We will be made complete in love. We can only love fully when we know how to minister to people who are suffering and need to know God. In this present world, love is given to overcome evil, not to avoid it. We worship a God who raises the dead. To die in Jesus Christ is to gain eternal life by eliminating all further suffering. It will all pass away! Christians who live by the world's standard of pleasure have compromised God's Word. All people have protective patterns to avoid suffering, which is a sign of the eternity we all long for. But it can't be received in this world with sin and evil present. God is fully acquainted with grief and sorrow, and that is why He paid the price of His Son dying on the cross. He promises a new life of comfort beyond comprehension in a glorified state where death can never happen again! He will carry all who believe in Him through the first death, bringing us to eternal life forever. All people contribute to the world's pain, and all have a chance to get off the hook of being separated from God forever, a glorious promise. Endure the pain, and don't let it stop you if you love Jesus. Rejoice in His salvation and reconciliation. You will be raised up and comforted forever.

The Peril of Money

On one side of the cross is the blessing of material provision from God and knowing what the word enough means. On the other side of the cross, we are warned against greed and the love of money that takes the place of the love of God in people's hearts. Luke 16:13 says we cannot serve both God and money. God warns us of the Peril of money. One of the three main temptations Satan tried to lay on Jesus was offering Him the kingdoms of the world if he would bow down and worship him. Having all you can get in the realm of material things is a lie from the Father of lies, the devil himself. There are two places where you are going to live.

Are you in the land of milk and honey? Or are you in the land of milking the money? The land of milk and honey means having enough provision from God to thrive in your soul and enjoy life by being grateful for all the good things God has provided for you. It does not lack what is really needed and brings contentment with what you have. It entails having enough food, clothing, a safe place to sleep, and a solid roof over your head. It is the freedom of watching out for debt which means you do not spend too much money without working for it first. It gives us the ability to enjoy our work and enough material things to share with people who can receive love and give love back. We will have a generous spirit and be willing to share, being satisfied and knowing Jesus gives us enough! If you're not living in this place, you may be living in the other place. The land of milking the money is the place where many people focus on consuming wealth as their main goal in life. They're going after the dream of power, comfort, and ease focused only on financially getting rich. Many rich people who have more money than they could need end up very unhappy because they have placed their trust in money. Trust is an issue of love. Love can only be shared with God and people. Money can't return love to you for it can only get you stuff that is not alive. You can't buy love from someone, and it will not make you happy if you think people will want you because you're wealthy financially. Houses, cars and boats, and diamonds are not breathing! Vacations and pleasures do not last. Without love, those things will get boring. Security comes from trusting in God and the risk of trusting in some people. Nothing will satisfy your life like a person you can trust in.

Alive and breathing with you in times of trouble and times of joy, love can only be explained in a relationship. There is much to learn from the scriptures on this topic. I came up with many scripture passages to place on each side of the cross to help you find the balance on how to live and be content knowing what enough is when it comes to money. Remember, trust that brings real security is only an issue with love, which requires two or more persons all the time. The only breathing thing a person can trust in that will cause them to fail is trusting in themselves or an atheist. Now let's look at the first side or the blessing side of these scriptures we should know. Take the time to read them, for they will help you to remove the idols you may have erected in your life from the lies of the dream to be rich in material blessings. The correct goal is loving God and knowing the purpose of money.

The land of milk and honey side of the cross is knowing what enough means and not falling to the power of greed and the love of money. It is knowing God will give you enough of what you need. Luke 10:30-37 read this and focus on verse 35. Proverbs 15:6, 2nd Cor.9:8-11, John 10:10, 1st Timothy 6:6-8, Deuteronomy 7: 12-15, Philippians 4:19, Proverbs 30:7-9, Proverbs 13:25, Matthew 6:25-34. The other side is the Peril of money. The danger that comes from the ones who are milking the money, or better said, trying to squeeze all they can get from the power of a greedy spirit. 1st Timothy 6: 8-10, Luke 12:13-21, Mathew16:26, Proverbs 28:20, 22, Proverbs 23:4, Eccl.5:10, Matthew 6:24, Hebrews 13:5, Revelation 3:17, Mark 10:17-27.

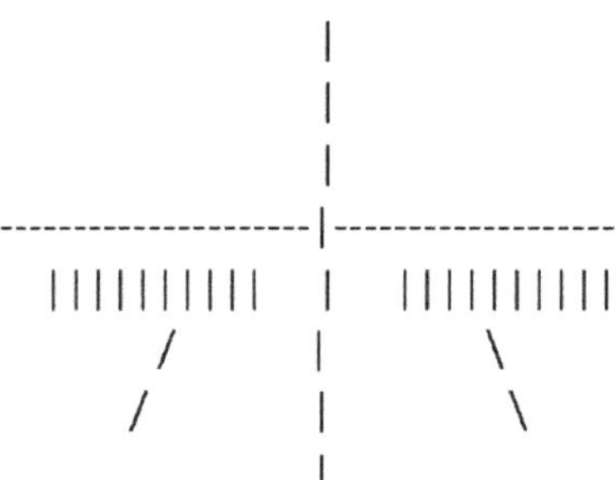

Love of money is evil
The peril of money
Idolatry replacing Gods
Love in a person's life

Love God First!
Know what enough
means! Contentment!
Worship God!

X +

Balance is keeping this side for our sanctification>>Love God!

We need God's side to keep the cross from falling down to the left side. The illustration above is an antithetical and honest evaluation of our deep attachment to money. Here are Scriptures for encouragement before leaving this topic of money. Proverbs 28:6 Better is the poor man whose walk is blameless in righteousness than the rich man who is crooked and perverse. Psalm 37:25, the righteous will never beg for bread or be unfed. Proverbs 13:25, the righteous has enough to satisfy his appetite, but the stomach of the wicked is in need. (Proverbs 28:22- A man with an evil eye hastens after wealth.) I want to share a poem I wrote. See Section Three- Overflow should Always Go!

Repentance is a gift by Option only!

Matthew 4:17--Repent is the first word Jesus said when He started His ministry to people. This came after He passed the testing of His love for God the Father in the wilderness, where the Spirit led Him to be tempted by the devil. If Jesus said Repent for the kingdom of heaven is at hand as the first words of ministry to people he encountered, then repentance can't be something God does for the ones He saves all by Himself. It puts the responsibility on the person to turn from their sin and ask God for forgiveness. That makes repentance a human responsibility, and God holds us to make that move toward Him.

Many in the church say repentance is a gift from God to the ones He intends to save. I would tell you that the option to repent and turn to God is a gift that must be practiced our entire life. It is a lifestyle by each Christian recognizing their need for a continual reconciliation to God through Jesus Christ. God requires each person to sincerely believe that He paid the price for all sin and to receive His work on the cross on their behalf. We must place our trust in Him and drop all the pride we have been living with by doing our own thing and thinking we can control our own life any way we want to.

We know we must enter the first death, and we can't save ourselves from that. We will not enter heaven unless we accept our Lord's great act of the substitutionary sacrifice by dying in our place. We can't say things like I hope God lets me in or I hope I have been good enough and that there is a heaven after this life. That is a way humans duck their responsibility and want to continue controlling their own life with them on the throne. We must not be blinded by lies and realize we are not good enough within ourselves and the sinful nature we have.

Repentance is necessary, as is trusting Jesus. When we see the Holiness of God face to face and the great humility He has taken upon Himself to save us, we will understand clearly how amazing His love is for all people.

Repent and let God save you. Bow to the King of Kings! Every knee will bow willingly or unwillingly, and you do not want to be in the second group! Balance comes with continual repentance.

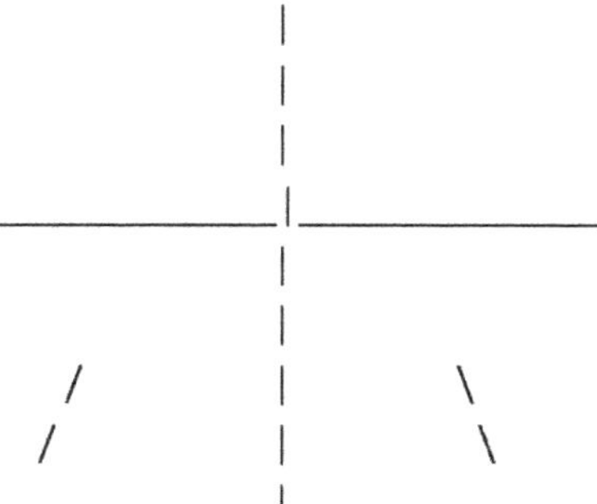

Repentance is not a gift from God without man's responsibility to turn to God by his action and choice Return to God in Humility!

God wants everyone to repent and live forever! The option to repent is a gift from God. We should make this correct choice! Crucial choice-choose life not death!

Live Here

+

Moving at Gods Pace-- in the Lord!

The pace of life changes when people realize God has come into their life and wants to lead them in the way they should choose and the things they should do. They know they are not supposed to be hasty anymore because we learn God's love that starts with patience. When we know we are not to be anxious for anything, some of us hesitate and become ambivalent. We can come to a point where we are unsure how to move with God, and we don't move when we should. Moving in faith and walking in love is something many must learn. Here are some scriptures on how being hasty will cause waste. Who has not heard at least once in their life that haste makes waste? One side of the cross on this issue is found in these verses:

Philippians 4:6. Be anxious for nothing but in everything by prayer and supplication with thanksgiving let your requests be made known to God.

Proverbs 21:5. The plans of the diligent lead surely to advantage, but everyone who is hasty comes surely to poverty.

Proverbs 29:20. Do you see a man who is hasty in his words? There is more hope for a fool than for him.

Proverbs 19:2 Desire without knowledge is not good—how much more will hasty feet miss the way! Who has not heard at least once in their life that He or She who hesitates is lost? The other side of the cross is in these verses.

Proverbs 6:10-11 A little sleep a little slumber, a little folding of the hands to rest and poverty will come on you like a thief and scarcity like a vagabond. Proverbs 10:4 Lazy hands make for poverty, but diligent hands bring wealth. Proverbs 14:23 All hard work brings profit, but mere talk leads to poverty.

Acts 10:19-20 While Peter was still thinking about the vision, The Holy Spirit said to him, Simon, three men are looking for you. So get up and go downstairs. Do not hesitate to go with them for I have sent them.

Acts 20:27 (Paul speaking) for I have not hesitated to proclaim to you the whole will of God.) To live with balance in this is not easy because we know we want God to lead us. We also know that a man's way is not in himself nor is it in a man who walks to direct his own steps.

See Jeremiah 10:23-24. Our flesh will fight to regain control, and it is not always easy to know God's direction for our lives all the time. PRAY!

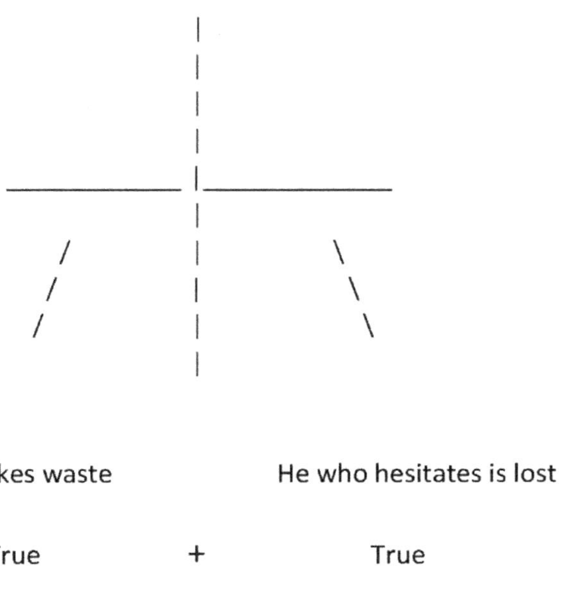

Haste makes waste He who hesitates is lost

True + True

Live here

Understanding from God's Perspective

We will look at this word from God's perspective by what we see in the scripture. There are two important sides to this word that most of us do not recognize, and I will tell you why we miss it. When we communicate with others as equal correspondents, we know it is important to establish an understanding with others in our close relationships. When we have a good understanding with other people, we have peace and the capacity for friendship. With God, we want to be called His friend, and we want intimacy with Him. We want understanding with God. The main difference between God and us, relationally speaking, is we are not equal correspondents. God created all men and women to be equal relationally but not equal with Him. That would not be possible. So God will speak to us in the scripture, knowing we are not equal, and tell us words like Trust in the Lord with all your heart and do not lean on your own understanding. In all your ways, acknowledge Him, and He will make your path straight.

Proverbs 3:5-6 is a familiar verse. There are two main components to understanding from God's perspective. We all know one of them much more than the other one. Comprehension is what we want and focus on whenever we hear the word understanding. Good comprehension with equal correspondents helps us create intimacy with our friends, and it is very good to understand the ones you love. You know where they are coming from and what to expect from them.

The other component of the word understanding is the one God wants to establish with us. Authority is the most important part of understanding from God's perspective. He knows we cannot be equal in our comprehension to His comprehension. His authority supersedes all our comprehension. His ways are much higher, and His thoughts are much higher. We will go through life without comprehension of many things, and that is why He tells us to trust in Him without leaning on our own understanding. What that means is we should not lean on our own authority over His authority. There will be times when we can't comprehend life, and in those times, we must not move out from under His authority. We are to stay under His authority and never demand explanations when we can't comprehend a situation.

I am not saying we never ask questions. I am saying be careful you do not demand answers from God. Job did this because of the evil that came upon him. He wanted a reason for the evil that was coming to Him. He received no explanation, but He got God's deliverance, love, and a double portion of blessing when it was over. Why does Job repent and put his hand over his mouth? Because he moved out from under God's authority demanding an explanation he would not get. With no comprehension, Job challenged God's authority. God says to him; you are finding fault with Me, the Almighty? Who is this who contends with the Almighty? Then Job repents and says I confess things that I did not understand. Things are too high and great for me to grasp. His confession was for moving out from under God's authority because he did not get comprehension.

After 14 WHY questions and stressful complaining, Job was in a position where he thought he was right and God was wrong. Job did not realize that evil has no logical comprehension and can't be explained. It is a malfunction of all good reasoning, purpose, and order. God will not have to explain to any of us regarding all the things that happen. We need His love and never to move out from under His authority. It all works out for good when we love Him PERIOD.

Psalm 111:10 tells us of the Authority factor superseding the comprehension factor of God's perspective on the word understanding. The fear of the Lord is the beginning of wisdom. A good understanding have all those WHO DO HIS COMMANDMENTS; His praise endures forever. From God's perspective, understanding means STANDING UNDER GOD!

Psalm 119:34--Give me understanding, that I may observe Your law and keep it with all my heart. Authority supersedes comprehension! This can apply in a smaller way with parents and their children. But sin and pride make this a real challenge in life. An example: take the garbage cans out, son, before you go to your game. Okay father, I will see you later. The son leaves without taking the garbage cans out for his father. He comprehended the request from his authority figure. But he did not stand under his authority figure. He did not obey. Maybe the son thought his dad could take it out just as easily as he could. Or maybe he forgot the request. The son comes home, and his dad says, why didn't you take the garbage cans out when I asked? The son may say I don't understand why I always have to do it. He is dismissing the authority factor in the situation. He is missing the most important part. Dads' authority factor supersedes the son's puzzled comprehension when dad is raising him and providing all his provisions until the son goes out on his own.

If the son was respectful and showed love to his father, he would do some things regardless of what he thinks or comprehends about the situation at home. We should stand under God's authority regardless of what we think or comprehend about any situation. We should also stand under in the times when we have no comprehension. We will be blessed. God's authority becomes the beauty of our reconciliation with Him. It is beautiful and secure to know we are safe forever with the (I AM) of the universe. My Father is not only the real God. He is the absolute Authority of the universe. When we don't understand by comprehension, we can stand under Him by the authority factor and know it will work out for good. We are loving Him by staying under Him! There is submission and obedience because of Who HE IS! This is the understanding God is looking for from us. This is loving God when we always stay under His authority. If evil breaks loose, as difficult as it may be, don't demand comprehension.

Ask God and check your approach. There may not be a logical answer. God will come through for us sooner or later while the test of faith is happening. Wait and do not demand an answer. Our correct responses of faith put us in the best position to get God's resolve when He acts to bring us relief. Remember this quip; God is our grief relief when we make Him our Chief! Here is the balance we can have for the cross is always a plus.

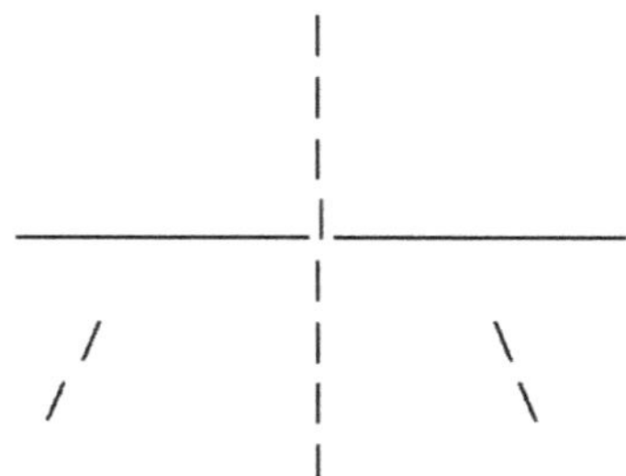

Understanding is God's Authority with our comprehension!

True

Both

Understanding is God's Authority without our comprehension. We stand under God always!

True

We live here +

1. Authority Supersedes-----------------I stand under Lord!
2. Comprehension------------------------I understand Lord!

+

The Cross is always a plus!

The peace that passes all comprehension is the peace that comes from standing under God!

Love and Good Deeds Always! Miracles on occasion

Acts 10:38 Here is where I discovered the importance of the plus words, which are the conjunctions joining all the information to study the scriptures in detail. We seek to get everything from what is being said to us by the Holy Spirit.

Acts 10:38 is a very informative scripture that should encourage every Christian of the Deity of Jesus Christ. It is written in a way that caught my attention. There are two distinct areas of ministry from the anointing of the Holy Spirit to bring to people who desperately need to be reconciled to God. I was asking myself why it was written the way it is. Here is the scripture: You know of Jesus of Nazareth, how God anointed Him with the Holy Spirit and with power, and how He went about doing good and healing all who were oppressed by the devil, for God was with Him. I see the word (and) used three times to connect two distinct activities of the Holy Spirit's anointing to represent the complete love of God. There is an anointing for the fruit of doing good which is equal to love in action. There is an anointing of power to heal and deliver people from the devil's bondage. Both are resurrection power God can give to those who follow Jesus and do His will. We need the fruit of love which is the fullness of God. (Ephesians 3:19).

When we love from God's anointing, it is a perfect love that changes people on the inside. The word power in this scripture comes from the added anointing of God to heal and deliver, which only God can do with His supernatural power. Miracles can happen through God's people, but I believe that going out and doing good deeds of love should be focused on first. Acts of love are for every day. The supernatural power that Jesus displayed was periodically chosen in certain situations to let people know God was in Jesus and Jesus was God. He loved people every day for the three and a half years He ministered on earth. He did many supernatural acts of healing and casting out demons, but they would not be considered one every day. That would amount to 1,275 supernatural acts of healing and deliverance He performed. If He chose to do one every day, we know He could.

The amount of good deeds in the anointing of love from the Holy Spirit done by Jesus in three and a half years would be hard to count. Just ten demonstrations of perfect love from Jesus each day would make that number 12,750 times He did an act of love to someone. He walked in love continuously, and the acts of kindness and generosity never stopped. He did the supernatural acts periodically as the Trinity chose and determined in each situation. When the scripture says Jesus went about doing good from the anointing of the Holy Spirit, we can come to an inference that it was every day. God is love! When we read the words >>-and healing all who were oppressed by the devil-<<-we can come to an inference it was when the situation was agreed upon by the Trinity to get involved in a way only God could! Some Christians act on this verse out of balance. Jesus showed many acts of love, all while He was growing up without a supernatural miracle. We know salvation happens every day, and babies are born every day. Many consider these two as miracles, and rightly so! Bible records show 37 Supernatural Miracles Jesus did in the Gospels. When Jesus went <u>about</u> doing good, He often incurred evil resistance. He had to go A-Bout with the devil many times and always won by KNOCK OUT! He didn't take any blows until He went to the cross and died in our place!

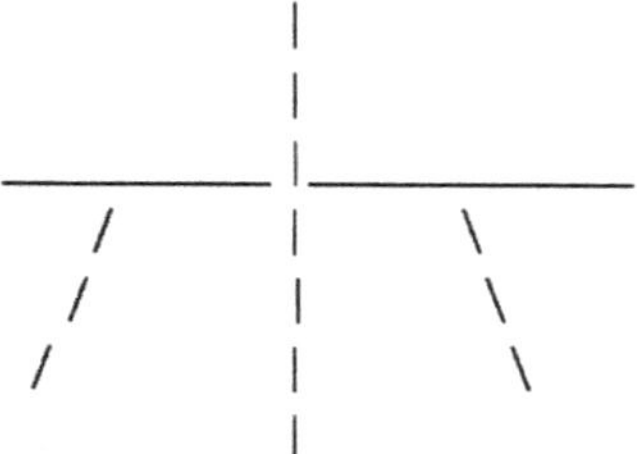

Christians should always practice love. Bible Miracles don't happen anymore. Just love people like Jesus did.

Christians should always practice love. Bible Miracles are equal to acts of love. We can do everything Jesus did!

Christians can do acts of love daily because the love of the Holy Spirit has been poured into their hearts. (Romans 5:5) all versions. Love should be practiced every day in little acts of kindness and in big ways to meet pressing and urgent needs! God can and will still do supernatural miracles periodically through some of the people He anoints with power. He knows the faithful and humble followers who love and obey His will. They are seeking to build His Kingdom on earth and giving God all the Glory He deserves!

Changes in Technology and how it is affecting the Church

Many people think it's a positive statement to say that technology is great and I can save so much time. Since you now have time to do other things, how are you spending that time? Your life has not been extended. None of our moment-by-moment existence is spent saving time. Time marches on, and you will be doing something else. If the technology age presents itself in many convenient ways, why are people saying remember the good old days?

We are told in the bible that dwelling on the past is not from wisdom. Eccl. 7:10.

God is the same yesterday, today, and forever! (Hebrews 13:8.)

So what has technology done to enhance our relationships with God, and what has it done to hinder our relationships with God? Many things are faster and easier to get done, and I will ask how does that help our character to become more like Jesus Christ? God wants to conform all people to the image of Jesus Christ by saving them through His wonderful reconciliation.

Is the church growing in the area of patience and perseverance? Love is patient, and it always perseveres.

Is technology motivating us to spend more of the time we say we are saving to spend more time bringing the gospel to the millions who need to hear it? The world believes in a fast day; people are often in a hurry!

God believes in a day too fast to stop all their scurry and worry! To give God attention is much more than a mention; when you're still before God, you will feel the ascension! God would like to have some of the time you have gained now that you spend less where you used to spend more.

I hear something much more now than I used to hear it years ago. I hear Christians say, okay, let's say a quick prayer. Technology can tempt many people to get in a hurry and get lazy and spoiled and much less relational and personal with others. I know of a woman who said she has a very good relationship with a person she has been texting and sending e-mails to and talking a little bit over the phone. He lives a thousand miles away. They have not met face to face and she told me you could have a good relationship with this kind of correspondence. I asked her how long she had been in this correspondence. She said two years, I met him online, and we hit it off. We can share our pictures on our smartphones. It is a great relationship? I think it would be better in a face-to-face reality where holding hands could bring some emotional stability. Holding hands is a gift from God and I can even imagine how a hug can do wonders! I have heard fathers say they got together with their sons to go out to a restaurant, and the sons were texting each other at the table.

Do you think they started by, at least, shaking hands? Examine your lives honestly and ask yourself how the convenience of technology can cause you to do God's will more often in the way He would like to see it done. Spend time in prayer. It is not outdated because you are enjoying your smartphones or wrapped up in the devil's plan to keep you moving so fast that you get exhausted. Find the balance we all need. Real intimacy comes from face-to-face fellowship. Facebook friends are only an acquaintance. Can you really help them in a time of need? Can they help you in a time of need? A very limited answer is all you can come up with. Spend two years in a face-to-face relationship with an unbeliever leading someone to Christ. The angels of God would give that a standing ovation, and so would Jesus!

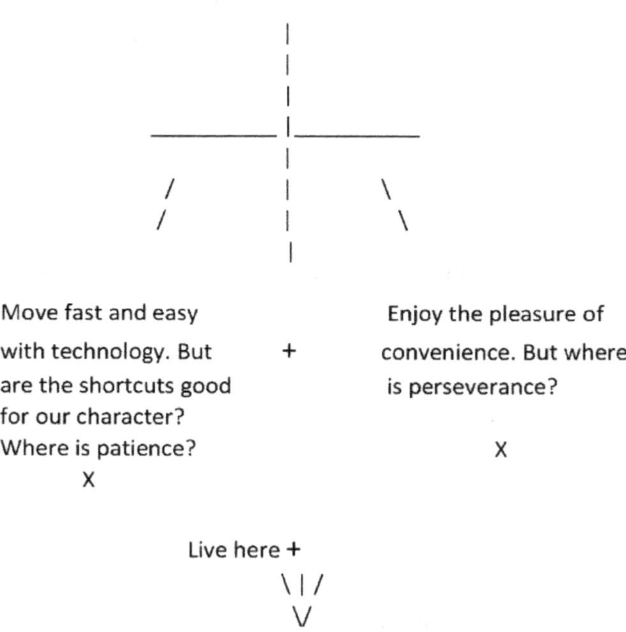

Keep pleasure and convenience limited. Be patient and use more of the time you have building relationships face to face. Lead other people to Jesus for salvation with your focus on being a minister of reconciliation. 2nd Corinthians 5:18. Cause a big party to happen in heaven! Luke15:10-Rejoice Forever! It is good to grasp one thing and not let go of the other. The man who fears God will avoid all extremes. Ecclesiastes 7:18 NIV

The Head and the Heart should never work apart!

The human anatomy must come together in the knowledge of knowing God personally and worshipping Him in the Spirit. There must be a stronger focus on our reconciliation than our religion. The one true religion is the reconciliation that brings us back to God through Christ, giving us regeneration from the Holy Spirit in our hearts and mind.

Titus 3:5, The cross is always a plus. + A new Heart from God in us + a new Mind from God in us = Being a real Christian! (Read Ezekiel 36:26-27 and 1st Corinthians 2:16.)

The church gets way out of balance when the head on our neck does not join our heart about 18 inches lower in location. We see great thinkers and rational people using the mind above all else, not showing deep compassion and expressing their feelings, thinking being emotional is always ignorant and immature. We see people who have received a new heart from God fail to draw on the new mind we have in Christ to help them attain the wisdom of exercising God's thoughts from the Spirit. The mind of Christ must be formed in us, and the heart of God must be formed in us with the love that surpasses all knowledge.

The head people (too much brain focus) can get prideful without the deep humility we need to serve God. The heart people (emotionally) can get out of balance by letting their feelings lead them with too much subjectivity. It is a complete renewing from the mind of Christ and a complete transformation from God's heart that gives us the fullness of love and eternal life. We should also think of the heart as the center of our whole being. It is not easy to comprehend how everything works together, but all of it must be synchronized the way only God can make it happen. We are being transformed into humility and holiness so we can live with God and do His will. The human mind can miss the way of the heart and mind of God. The human heart is sick and wicked, and it can miss the way of the heart and mind of God. The mind of the flesh is an enemy of God. The heart of the flesh is filled with the corruption we have received from the fall of man and the flesh nature of Satan. Our goal is love from a pure heart, a good conscience, and a sincere faith.

1st Timothy 1:5. A pure heart never dismisses the mind of Christ and the thoughts of the Spirit. Love is a choice and not a feeling. Love is an action choosing to do kind acts and good deeds and not to do evil. Love is a heart of compassion, mercy, and grace. Grace is a gift from God that instructs us to choose sensible actions and wise choices and to walk in the righteousness of Jesus Christ. (Titus 3:11:12).

The mind and the heart should never stop working together, for that's the only way we can receive God's greatest commandment.

Matthew 22: 37, YOU SHALL LOVE THE LORD YOUR GOD WITH ALL YOUR HEART, AND WITH ALL YOUR SOUL, AND WITH ALL YOUR MIND.

This is the greatest commandment. The best way to put it may be to say we love God reciprocally with our whole being. Our bodies are the temples of the Holy Spirit. 1st Corinthians 6:19. Our invisible makeup is our spirit, mind, will, and emotions, and there is no need to debate the differences in opinions on the soul and spirit.

We think, we feel, we choose, and we have a heart and mind and a brain that passes the invisible messages of communication. It stores knowledge, and it is beyond our imagination and comprehension when we see how good God has been by creating us the way He has done it! Amazingly, we are made in God's Image, and He says we are wonderfully made and were created for fellowship with Him. We Love Him wholeheartedly, and the head and heart must never work apart. It is obvious when they don't work together that, there will be problems. People are destroyed for lack of knowledge. People are hated for a wicked heart. The Lord could only save us all by the necessity of the cross. He has paid a tremendous price for the poison of sin and pride that came upon His wonderful creation of man and woman, whom He said was very good! When we look at all of our characteristics and the functions we can do, we can be forever grateful. God has come to restore His most important part of His creation; people made in His Image and destined for eternity with Him. We must love Him with our whole being. It is only now, as Christians, that we can!

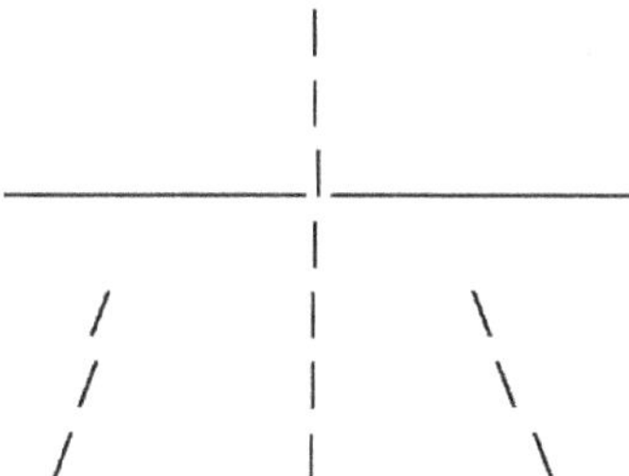

My head knowledge of God is enough. It makes an objective thinker. it guides me in faith as Christian child of God.

X

I serve God from my heart and that's enough. Real Faith is demonstrated in heart knowledge.

X

Live here!

+

Both head and heart, our whole being must love God! We should live in obedience to Matthew 22:37. Loving God with all our heart, soul, and mind!

Mercy and Grace is a Two Fold Help Package

This is the most complete witness for the Lord; showing Mercy and Grace is a twofold help package that can be delivered to unbelievers at the same time. I believe we should show them both together. We have been taught that God's mercy does not render the due penalty. It is compassion to let a person off the hook and withhold the deserved punishment. Grace is the favor God shows to people who do not deserve it, for they have sinned against Him or other people. When we look at Hebrews 4:16, we see a familiar passage of scripture. Many people have quoted it and know it to be a popular verse. Hebrews 4:16 is clearly a +Cross is always a plus scripture.+ It says- Therefore let us draw near with confidence to the throne of grace, so that we may receive mercy <u>and</u> (the plus+ word) find grace to help in time of need. Do you see the order of how God works in this verse?

Mercy is received first at the throne of grace. Mercy is the prerequisite for grace. The wrath of our Holy Father had to be appeased first before He could show mercy and grace to follow. The first of four main works of the cross is the propitiation of God in the death and resurrection of Jesus. The Father put all His wrath on Jesus as our sin-bearer. The Holy of Holies was opened up to all who will come to God through the appeal of Jesus Christ. This is tremendous love of another kind. Having His Holiness satisfied, the Father will let every person who comes to Christ sit in the mercy seat. We are seated with God forever because of Jesus, our Lord, and Savior. The mercy seat comes before the heart and hand of God's grace. The other three main works of the Father at the cross are Redemption, Justification, and Reconciliation. Christians are reconciled in Jesus Christ, and we have received all four of these main works. They are appropriated to us as God's Born again Children. The last of the four works, our reconciliation to God, is the goal we have for other people to receive. This is what seals salvation for all people. We have become ministers of reconciliation; 2nd Corinthians 5:18. Our ministry can only be effective if we combine mercy and grace like we see in Hebrews 4:16. If we can't dismiss the sin from the sinner, how can we bring the Grace of God to others? We have to go past their sins like God went past ours before we can administer effective grace. The order is listed, and it is clear. Can I bring grace that saves people if I judge them from my mind and heart? The sin must always be separated from the sinner so we can see the person through the eyes of God's love for them.

I experienced God's mercy and grace once while delivering pizzas at Christmas. I was losing my business and needed some extra money. I rolled through a stop sign because business was backed up. The house was four houses left of the stop sign. I pulled into the driveway of my delivery, and a police car pulled into the driveway right next to me. The customer seeing the squad car flashing away was standing in the window looking out to see what was happening. It was an embarrassing situation, to say the least. I confessed to the police officer that I was wrong and how busy it was. I told him I should have stopped. It only takes three seconds. He let me off the hook and said alright, slow down and stop at the signs. I said thank you, officer. I received mercy for I was guilty and deserved a ticket.

Meanwhile, I have the customer in the window, and I have to bring six pizzas to him. He was having a party, and there were a lot of happy kids ready for their pizza. It took less than a minute to bring the pizzas in. I had two bags of three each and was good at carrying them. I told him the bill was 139 dollars. He gave me a check, and I said thank you without looking at the check. In the car, I looked to make sure the amount was at least 139 dollars. He wrote it out for 180 dollars and gave me a 41 dollar tip, and, boy oh boy, how the grace of God followed the mercy I had just received! It was a two-fold help package indeed! We do have an amazing God who loves us beyond our human comprehension. I had asked for mercy before I conversed with the police officer. I was not expecting God would lavish His grace at the same time. This was a very small example of the real benefits of God's mercy and grace. God's preference is for mercy over the judgment that could separate us from His love forever. We must bring His great love and salvation to others out of great gratitude for what He has done for us. Vessels of mercy or vessels of wrath, be glad you're not the latter! We are vessels of mercy for honorable use to save vessels of wrath from destruction!

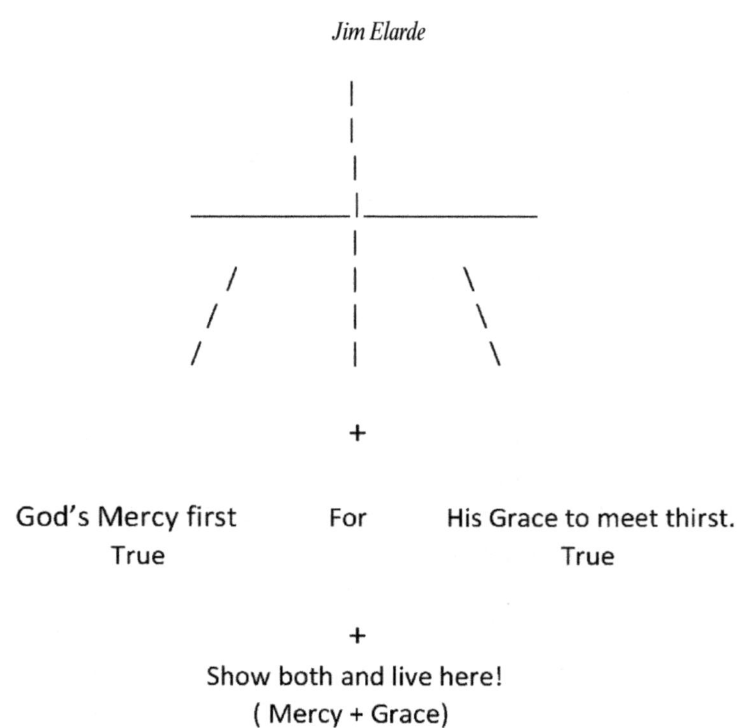

God's Mercy first For His Grace to meet thirst.
True True

\+
Show both and live here!
(Mercy + Grace)

God's Election for All to be Saved!

God says His choice to save us came before creation. That certainly tells us He knows the future, for He is eternal and not subject to time as we know it. God says more than once in scripture that He called people and knew people before the foundation of the world. Many call this desire of God His Election.

The church is divided on how they interpret our salvation results. We know that many are saved, and many will not be saved from the truth of scripture. There is a double predestination group that says God is responsible for saving the ones He wants to be saved and creating some who never get saved. But what stops them from salvation? This needs correct interpretation. It cannot be they had no choice to come to God through the promise or the appeal of Jesus Christ. They were not stuck with the wickedness of the fall without a choice to get out. I would not want a God who is tagged with the responsibility for some people being lost forever. That would contradict many scriptures that tell us of His equality of love for mankind and how He does not have any favorites when it comes to people. God does not want any person to be without salvation.

If it seems like God gets closer to some people more than others, it is because of the people's responses to Him. A humble yes enters us into the presence of God, and a prideful no will keep us away! Every man or woman is responsible for seeking God, and they will find Him! Another group from the overall church believes that the reason people do not get saved is all their own fault, and they willfully choose to reject God or Jesus Christ. They put all the responsibility on man to come to God and say man is without excuse. They are very close to the right balance of the truth. But they say we must work to keep our salvation once we receive it.

Remember the thief on the cross? They are reducing the fact it is God who does good works through us by His Spirit. They say we can lose salvation after we receive it. We can only lose intimacy in our loving relationship when we do not respond correctly by our obedience after salvation. Once we are a child of God through redemption, we are forever a child of God. How close we get to God depends on our responses of real faith, and He gave us the Holy Spirit to guide us to the correct responses.

We know salvation is a gift from God's mercy and grace, and that is written many times in scripture. Titus 3:4-7, Ephesians 2:8-10, and John 3:16 are three of many.

Humans can't earn or keep their way to heaven by good works. Through the works of the law, no man will be justified. (Galatians 2:16b)

John 6:40 makes it very clear that there has to be a correct response. Whoever believes in the gift God sent can be saved. It means whoever will trust in the work of Jesus Christ dying in their place for the wrong things all people have done. God is not wishing or wanting any people to perish but for all people to repent.

2nd Peter 3:9. We recognize the sin in us and show remorse and true contrition. We humble ourselves before God, knowing He is loving and forgiving us in Christ. We confess with our mouths and believe in our hearts that we need to be saved. I would like to say to all people that you are up for election to the kingdom of God. The potential of the power of the cross is for everyone. He paid the price for all human sin. All the names of all the people who ever lived were put into the election bowl of God's heart and mind. He intended an appointment for all people to the kingdom of God, and we are in the position to say I will keep my appointment. A humble Yes to God is required! Some people will cancel their appointment and say no. I will not bow down and serve anyone. I will be in charge of my own life and do it my way. They have the free will to make valid or foolish choices, and God will not force His love on one who says no to it. God will have to remove some names from his election bowl because some people canceled their appointment. This is my illustration of how things are. The scripture verifies it in a better and more convincing way.

In Revelation 3:5, Jesus says whoever overcomes by faith in Him will not have their name erased from the book of life. Jesus will erase some names from the book of life, meaning they were written or intended to be there ahead of time for salvation to belong to them. All people were in the mind and heart of God's love! Do you know you have been created to live in the kingdom of God? What is your response to this wonderful privilege and honor? Your name is written in the book of life- (God's mind and heart), and God does not want to erase it. You must run for the highest office where God is in charge of everything to get elected! Run to God's authority, for He is Lord of heaven and earth. Become His child and servant and live forever with Him in all His glory!

For the prideful people who say no to God, Proverbs 14:12 says there is a way that seems right to a man, but its end is the way of death. I would suggest to all men and women who do it all their own way to get up from their death bed and grasp the eternal life that is waiting for them. They will be forever grateful and forever alive! In Christ is the only hope for glory! All man's good works must be empowered by the Holy Spirit. We submit to His power after He is given to us through salvation in regard to the obedience of faith. Rom. 1:5.

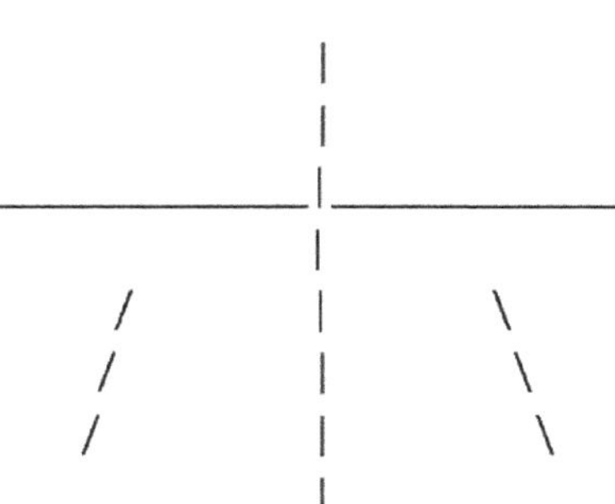

God predestined some people to be saved and some to be lost and separated from Him forever. X?

God holds everyone responsible to repent and say yes to His gift of salvation. But man has to work to keep it or he will be separated from God forever. X?

Live here +

Read the Balanced Explanation for a solid interpretation.

Balanced Explanation: God holds every person responsible to repent and say yes to the salvation that He has for them. They must be humble and show contrition, remorse, and a change of mind. They place their trust in Him! They receive the Holy Spirit and the calling to do the work of God by God's power in them. It is not by man's own strength in human flesh. If a man responds correctly in obedient faith, God will be allowed to do His will freely and for His pleasure in the faithful servant, He has saved. If the servant or the new redeemed child of God does not cooperate with God, he will lose the intimate fellowship God wants with him. Being a child by redemption, God will never take salvation away from one whom He has saved. That would make salvation something we have to earn to keep.

We would be nullifying the mercy and grace of God, who says we can never be separated from the love of God in Christ and nothing can separate us after He has saved us once; Romans 8:37-39. We can lose intimacy by not obeying God's word and not cooperating. God gets the glory for every good work a Christian does by the Holy Spirit. He knows any work of the flesh has the wrong motive and is worthless before God's eyes. We can delay our sanctification by sin and disobedience, but we will never be thrown out of our adopted state as a blood-bought child of God. God will finish the work He started in every Christian, even if He has to take His child home earlier because of sin. 1 Cor.5:5. The presence of sin is not completely gone till we are glorified!

Fighting Temptation God's Way

Temptation tries to attack us and never asks for permission. It does not say Knock, Knock, can I tempt you with sin? It comes through the door without knocking or asking many times. The devil is a very rude intruder that wants to steal, kill, and destroy. He wants us to doubt God. He wants us to be discouraged. He wants us to be diverted, and he wants us to be delayed. He wants us to be divided and he wants us to be defeated. He is the adversary of our soul. I remember a time after my conversion to Christ when I was hit hard with temptation. I felt like I was frozen and stopped in my tracks. Then I called on God. God came through, but it was difficult because of the deeply ingrained sin habits we have in our fallen nature. The internal war goes on, and whoever wants to live godly in Christ will be tempted. Evil intrusion will always try to get in the way of God's intended will for our lives. In the Lord's Prayer, we pray and ask the Father to lead us not into temptation but to deliver us from evil. Deliver us from evil means; Lord, help us escape when it comes or help us not to cross the line.

When we are honest, we can also pray, Lord, keep me from evil so that I may not cause pain to someone else. The absence of denial is a good thing to have. It keeps us from the delusion that we are just fine! Paul said in Romans 7:18 For I know that nothing good dwells in me, that is, in my flesh.

Another writer has said we could ask God to keep us out of the bait shop, so we don't come up with the hook! But the hook will be trying to snare us as long as we are still in these fallen earthly bodies. There is one thing we must agree on with temptation. God will test us out by allowing it. By the Holy Spirit, God led Jesus into the wilderness for 40 days to be tempted by the devil. Jesus was tested before His ministry started, and we all know of the three temptations where He defeated the devil, and the devil had to depart to tempt someone much weaker. God is going to test us when we are his disciples. So we come to the correct focus on dealing with temptation, learning to get victory over it in a direct conflict, and abiding and believing in the Word of God.

We start with Jesus's example in Matthew 4:1-11. We learn three areas of temptation we are all going to go through. These are the areas where we will have to face it head-on. When we are hungry for bread or any blessing, we can trust God's word to provide what we need at the right time. If we serve our flesh when the time is not right, we are not trusting the Lord. We get hungry for something, but we never steal or covet. We live by His promise to take care of us and that the righteous are never in a position where they should beg. We also learn never to test God by trying to demand an intervention by putting ourselves in a dangerous position. We never try to control God in anything. This temptation comes to us, and we hardly recognize it. We vie for control from the poison of pride in us from the fall and Satan himself. Never try to manipulate God to do something miraculous or test Him to prove Himself. Satan was talking to God as if he was an equal correspondent in presenting this temptation. What a fool the devil is! We will also be tempted toward the love of money and power by the world's standards. We must pass this test, for it is one of the hardest, along with sexual temptation. We are hybrids on the highway to heaven, and we must keep our eyes off all the billboards along the side of the highway that promote the temporary pleasures of this fallen world. Many of them promote the love of money and sex, which you see and hear about almost every day. We can't wear a blindfold when we are traveling on the highway to heaven. Looking straight ahead is better advice than we realize! (Proverbs 4:25-27)

A glance does not bend the neck to the right or left, but a gaze causes some of us to think we are an Owl! More than a few auto accidents have happened from people who thought they were Owls! God promises we have an escape when we are tempted.

1 Corinthians 10:13 speaks of our escape. No temptation has overtaken you but such as is common to man; and God is faithful, who will not allow you to be tempted beyond what you are able, but with the temptation will provide the way of escape also, that you may be able to endure it. We can never stand by ourselves, and we will always depend on God for the victory we can experience in Jesus Christ, our Lord, and Savior. When we sincerely ask God, He promises to help us run from temptation. When we do not run or nip it in the bud, we will ponder to engage in it. When we cross the line with the mind of the flesh, we will sin and settle for a brief moment of pleasure that will leave us empty afterward.

James 1:14-15 says each one is tempted when he is carried away by his own lust. Then when lust is conceived, it gives birth to sin, and when sin is accomplished, it brings forth death. God says He will help when we want Him to. We can learn to run to God, calling on His power to keep us from sin. We have the choice to do so. It is better than pretending God is absent from the situation and trying to hide in the sin. Many times, we realize how much Jesus had to come to die in our place and how the gravity of sin had no other solution. We appreciate Him all the more when we see who we are in our flesh nature apart from Him. We can agree with the Lord and realize that there was no other way but for God to do it all the way He did. Amazing love, how can it be that Jesus came to die for me! The battle may take a long time, but we will have complete victory in Jesus. The remedy for pride is a slow but sure process that God will finish in us. He who began a good work in us will perfect it until the day of Christ Jesus. (Philippians 1:6) and the God of all grace who called us to His eternal glory in Christ will Himself perfect, confirm, strengthen and establish us. (1 Peter 5:10) God will help us to resist the temptations, and we will come to agree with Him by the power of His love for us! We will give Him all the glory! Read 2 Peter 2:9

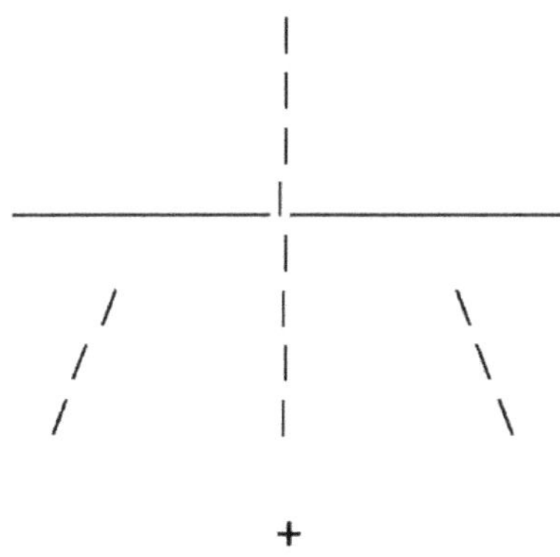

Fight temptation with the Word of God when you are in direct conflict with it.

True

Fight temptation with God's promise for you to escape and run to God from the temptation!

True

Live here +

The Balance of the Cross is always a plus!

Overlook the Transgressions of others in Two Ways

We want balance in dealing with love that will overlook an offense. Proverbs 10:12- Love covers a multitude of sins or many transgressions. Proverbs 19:11- A man's discretion makes him slow to anger, and it is his glory to overlook a transgression. Ephesians 4:15- but speaking the truth in love, we are to grow up in the Love of Christ who is our Lord. If I were to tell you God wants us to overlook other people's transgressions, how would you define the word overlook? Webster defines it in a very complete way.

1. To look over: INSPECT
2. To look down upon from above
3. To look PAST: miss, IGNORE, or EXCUSE
4. To SUPERINTEND, OVERSEE.

We can focus on these capitalized words and practice love in our relationships by overlooking a transgression. To Ignore or Excuse and look Past go together and Inspect, Superintend and Oversee all go together. Suppose you are married, and you know that means love is unconditional. Growing a strong relationship means knowing when to ignore or excuse your partners' offenses against you. It is also knowing when to confront the offense in a gentle way, to resolve issues, and bring trust, unconditional acceptance, and maturity in love. We must love past many sins that we all have and work to correct the ones that need to be addressed. How critical it is to know this boundary and build upon it. The gentle approach is always in place. You can't get started if you ruffle your partner's feathers.

We get out of balance when we ignore or excuse the transgressions that are too repetitive in each other. We will not get close by never taking the role of the Superintendent, the Overseer, or the love Inspector. On the other hand, bringing up every little thing without taking the role of the one who can look past and ignore some things can have someone walking on needles and pins or broken glass. No one can be comfortable with a perfectionist. No one should be too demanding and trying to hit a moving target.

We must always ask God for help in the most precious relationships He gives us, for they come from His incredible favor and from His mercy and grace. Knowing God's instructions on love to one another from His word and doing them will bring success in our relationships. Taking time alone with God is vital to any real good relationship, and His definition of love is not impossible for us to accomplish with each other. Love is patient. Watch out for the fast pace of our culture and the hurry and scurry I mentioned in the illustration on the effects of technology.

Patience must be present in love relationships, or it would not have been listed first in 1 Corinthians 13:4-8A. NIV, love is patient. Also, love is kind, and it does not envy, it does not boast, it is not proud. (Humility first for love to meet thirst!) Love is not rude, it is not self-seeking, it is not easily angered, and it keeps no record of wrongs. Do not keep a list of sins!

Do not allow an unforgiving attitude or carry a bitter spirit. Love does not delight in evil but rejoices with the truth. It always protects (Men be brave and always protect). All women like the warrior who can save the princess. Love always trusts (start with God and make sure it filters down!) Love always hopes; it never quits hoping in the anchor of our soul, Jesus. (Hebrews 6:19)

Love always perseveres. My earthly father would often say when we drove to work together, we have to keep on going! I remember his words and apply them to my walk with my Heavenly Father and the Lord Jesus as a Christian child of God. Overlook the transgressions of others. Know when to look PAST, IGNORE and EXCUSE them, and know when to SUPERINTEND, OVERSEE and be the LOVE INSPECTOR! Trust God because Love never fails.

God's Spirit and love has been poured out within our hearts as Christians who can bring His Love to all people. (Romans 5:5)

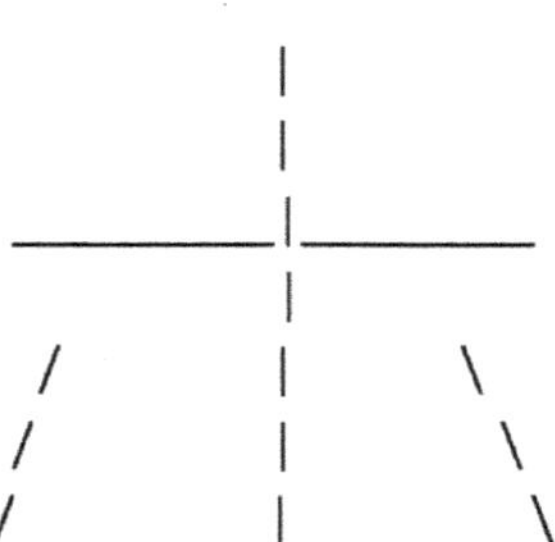

Active forgiveness!

+

+

Love looks past sins and offenses. Love excuses and ignores sin and offense some of the time without a word mentioned.

True

Active reconciliation!

+

Love superintends the relationship. Love oversees the relationship. We must be love inspectors to bear good fruit. Love corrects things and overcomes in God Way!

True

Balance live here + and grow in love!

We all need both sides for love to succeed!

Be—Come > the Righteousness of God in Christ

Regarding the righteousness we have received in Jesus Christ, 2nd Corinthians 5:21 says, He (God) made Him, (Jesus) who knew no sin to be sin on our behalf, that we might become the righteousness of God in Him. In some churches, I have seen what I believe is an imbalanced view of our righteousness in Christ from this scripture. We will focus on the word we, the word might, and the word become. The word we in this scripture is to be inclusive for its potential to reach all people. Paul is talking to the church at Corinth. But while he is writing, there will be more people coming into the kingdom by receiving Christ, so the (we) should be expanded to apply to all people who are yet to be saved. God wants all to be saved and would like all people to have their own Bible and to be reading this very wonderful scripture. Many call it the great exchange verse, where Christians exchange their sin for God's righteousness.

There could never be a better deal! Eternal life instead of eternal death and living a life of reconciliation to God in place of alienation from God forever. The next word is might. The word might shows less probability or possibility than the words (they will) would. This is saying many can get this great offer, but there is a condition where they may not. That a person might get saved is not a conclusion. They will have to trust in the salvation appeal of Jesus Christ. For the Christian who already has been saved, we will now focus on the last word underlined, become. It is easy to see the two words that are in this one word. Be and come tells me one is now and the other is for later. For me to (be) is currently happening. This is an easy way to see the position of the righteousness we, who are saved, have received. Righteousness is positional before it is completely accomplished. There is more to come.

There will be the progressive sanctification of the Holy Spirit doing the transformation and conforming us to the image of Jesus Christ. It is Christ in you, the hope of glory. (Colossians 1:27)

Glory is a promise, and God can not lie! Glorified is a hope and not a fact until we are through with our earthly bodies of sin. Some of the churches are out of balance in their teaching. I have heard more than a few times over the years that we can't get any more righteous than we are as soon as we are saved. They are speaking God's promises to complete our sanctification, but that can promote complacency in the believers to rest in their positional righteousness. They may not cooperate with God in the process of being renewed and transformed and growing up in the love of Christ into a mature man or woman.

A person can be sluffing off or causing too much delay in their progressive righteousness. The delays often start from the devil! We do have levels of growth in our walk with God. We can have an unequal yoke with another Christian, and we are not all in the same place on our journey. This shallow teaching is like saying since God sees me finished in my sanctification, I will not feel too bad when I stumble or sin, for it is under the blood. It brings us back to Romans 6:1-2, May it never be that I continue in sin! We are supposed to hunger and thirst after righteousness. Jesus said this in Matthew 5:6. Do we lose our hunger and thirst at the beginning of our salvation? That is a sure road to backsliding right back into the world! Please, whoever you are and wherever you are teaching someone, don't tell the new believer they can't get any more righteous than they are as soon as they become a new Christian. To be new in salvation is a privileged position, not a finished one, until a huge amount of righteousness arrives in Christ being formed in us! The body of sin dies daily. Galatians 4:19 >> Paul is saying, my children with whom I am again in labor until Christ is formed in you.

Until is not a present word. It proves there is much that has to come! I pray until I get God's answers, even if I do not get some of the answers at all. Until is a keyword for Christians to have embedded in their minds and heart. Are we having any trouble with waiting for more of God's righteousness? I would say to you, don't quit praying and hungering for it! We will be made completely righteous in Christ for all of eternity! For now, it's Christ in you, the hope of glory. When we are finished, it will be hope changed to the fact that glorification has taken place.

BE + Come = Our Righteousness in God!

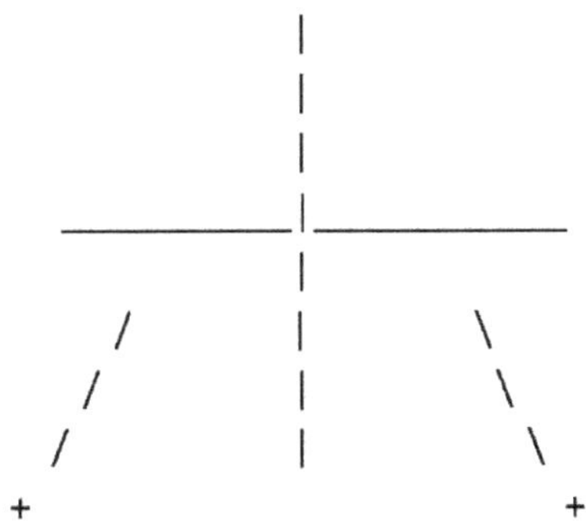

BE	+	COME
Positional Righteousness Salvation has started God will finish it in us!		Progressive Righteousness Our sanctification is in process. We will made complete and glorified!
True		True

+

Live in balance here!

Forgiveness and Reconciliation + We do both

In all our relationships with people, forgiveness is a choice that agrees with God and His nature. We can forgive someone without listening to our wounded emotions as long as we want to agree with God, who has paid the price to establish forgiveness. As a matter of fact, God's forgiveness fills the atmosphere. When Jesus was raised from the dead, forgiveness manifested everywhere and is ready to make its way into anyone's heart. We will start with the fact that God has forgiven all the sins that have ever been committed. Every sin is under the blood of Jesus, and forgiveness is available to all people. All have sinned and fall short of the glory of God (Romans 3:23.)

In Matthew 6:14-15, Right after the Lord's Prayer, Jesus speaks of the importance of forgiveness, For if you forgive men for their transgressions, your heavenly Father will also forgive you. But your Father will not forgive you if you do not forgive other people. Believers read this, and we should know how to interpret it correctly. If we don't forgive others, we deny our common ground as sinners who need God's forgiveness. Everyone is in continual need of forgiveness. The first condition for forgiveness to be appropriated to us is to receive God's forgiveness through salvation. Reconciliation can only take place when we appropriate forgiveness by repentance from our sins and humbly trusting in Christ for our salvation. Forgiveness from God is only imputed by reconciliation, which is the completed work of the cross. Both must happen. All people are forgiven, but all people are not reconciled. With no reconciliation, a person will not be saved. Head knowledge of God forgiving us in Christ will not be enough. Jesus saved us to bring us back into the relationship we are supposed to have with God. Talking to His disciples, Jesus also let them know they must forgive others to ensure they keep the manifestation of the freedom that comes to believers when we repent of our ongoing sins.

We can't live by harboring unforgiveness toward someone and experience the freedom that we need. A Christian is warned in scripture against bitterness in the heart. (Hebrews 12:15.)

We must practice forgiving others as a new way of life in Christ. God forgave us to regain involvement with us relationally. The enmity we had has been removed. We need to forgive others and make an effort to be involved with them whenever it's possible. God would like us to reconcile every broken relationship, if possible, and establish peace. Our peaceful involvement with them is the best proof of releasing forgiveness to others. Realize the difference between forgiveness with reconciliation compared to forgiveness without reconciliation.

There are times when believers are in situations where they can't be reconciled to others. The person may have died or moved far from you, or they may have chosen to keep a permanent distance from you. We can do our part by choosing to forgive them in our new heart from God. We should know if we are showing unforgiveness toward someone or if we have a bitter spirit in us. There are people we can't reconcile with because they may not be pursuing God and we are pursuing God. They may have told you that your Jesus stuff is not for them! We can't reunite with a toxic relationship, but we can do our part to forgive and pray for them. We need the wisdom to know what is best for us to retain a healthy relationship with God first and foremost. It is hard when we think of people who treated us poorly or disrespected us. We need to pray for them and not let the thought of them cause us to rejoice that they are gone from our lives. It's better to pray and hope for God to heal them and save them if they are unbelievers. If we know a Christian who was not a good yoke for us, we can still pray but stay away. We must keep our hearts guarded at all times. (Proverbs 4:23)

When we often feel an evident dislike for a person we did not get along with, we can go against our instincts and pray for these people in our past. Remember that we also have done things to offend others, and we can stop pointing the finger at the offenses of others. Confession of our sins with a regular examination of our own heart before God will keep it guarded against one of your worst enemies, yourself! I say to you what I heard many times: Let God slay the Philistine who is in you! He may be a giant! Forgiveness to others does not mean forgetting what happened or the person who offended you. It may take a good amount of time for the pain of the offense to be healed. A divorce is a great example of this. Divorce is an evil circumstance to absorb, and God hates it very much. But if you married without God's involvement and you were not a Christian, you may balance the situation out for the good side of it. God can use it to get a hold of you. It can help a person come to God with a traumatic experience like divorce. I went through one as an unbeliever, and now I found my true love! God the Father, Son, and Holy Spirit gave me all the love I was looking for! God poured His love into my heart forever! Nothing can separate me from His love. (Romans 8:38-39). Another issue on forgiveness is to make sure you know how to forgive yourself when you recognize you are living in Romans the 7th Chapter. Thank God for Jesus, who will deliver us from this body of sin! We must forgive ourselves without excusing the behavior that can come out of us. No condemnation + go and sin no more! Fight the good fight of faith and love God and people. You can forgive and love even the people you can't seem to like. Ask God for mercy and grace to help you toward the goal of His love! We reciprocate love to God by loving others. Forgiveness will be a constant practice as long as we are in our earthly bodies that must be transformed to the likeness of Christ. We owe love to God and others, and love is never without forgiveness in this present life. Have you ever thought of the freedom we will have from being without sin and the need for forgiveness? The freedom of perfect love flowing for all eternity from the completeness of being conformed into the image of Jesus! Wow! What a blessing to know it is coming! Amen!

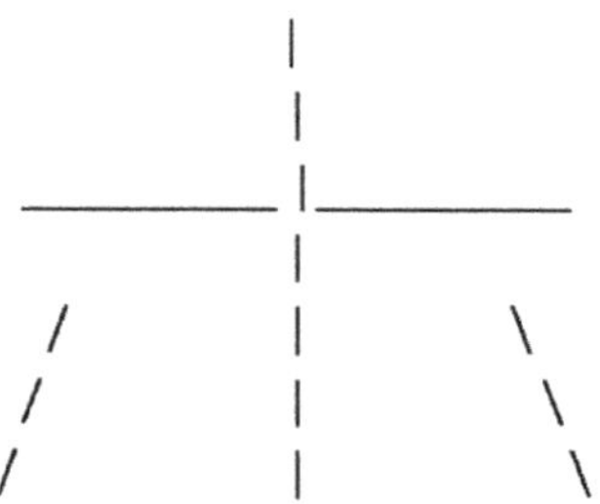

Forgiveness is necessary to keep us free when reconciliation is not possible. We can pray for the people who need salvation and all Christians who need to be healed who are choosing separation from their partner.	Forgiveness is necessary and must be with reconciliation to God in Christ for our salvation to take place. We can have involvement with many people we forgive to make our forgiveness a sure witness of God's desire.
+	+
True	True with reconciliation!

+

Live here with both sides in balance.

Fallen Creatures and Responsible Persons Cry for Mercy!

Look at the human condition with an honest evaluation. The wonders of the human body and the abilities God has given people made in His image often seem amazing. At the same time, look at the things people do against one another and the problem of evil in the world. Hatred and strife, and selfishness are present. An honest evaluation of man is He is a fallen creature and not always able to perform morally upright. He is made in God's image, and he is a responsible person who is accountable for his actions. The word of God is very true about what happened in the beginning. Man inherited the nature of Satan when Adam and Eve fell in disobedience. Life was perfect for them until they were deceived. God held them completely responsible for their wrong actions, and He had to put the curse on mankind.

All creation was subject to the fall because man was put in charge of a perfect creation. We now have a man who is no longer perfect, so now he has to deal with imperfections in creation. Our responsible man became a helpless creature, and death spread into the world. God never stopped loving them and always had a backup plan knowing they could fall. They had a valid choice to prove their love to God, but they chose pride and deception. God did not cause them to fall, for He is eternal and can see the future and all the choices people are going to make. God tested them for their loyalty. Looking at how we are made and our ability to choose, feel, think and relate to each other, you know that love is a choice, not an automatic response.

There was no validity for God to make a man who could not prove his faithfulness to His creator. We all choose freely, and that is what makes us so wonderfully made. We are created to act responsibly and rule all the things on earth. We all want the love of our creator, but we have the spirit of rebellion inside of us. There are good things to say about life and the privilege we have to be alive, and all of us would like to live forever and enjoy prosperity in our souls.

Death is an intruder that came when the devil was thrown out of heaven as the author of evil. One-third of Gods created angels took part in an insurrection led by Satan. God took all His nature of goodness, holiness, and love from them. It resulted in their eternal separation from God. Man can do great things to show his creator's unique goodness and ability. Man is like the devil in his cursed nature, capable of doing very bad things. We know God made man righteous, but man has sought out many devices. (Eccl. 7:29)

Our eternal Holy God will always exist in moral perfection. We will see Him in judgment one day. All who believe in His Son, Jesus Christ, will enter heaven after the first death. They will be resurrected to an eternal body that can never die! Those who reject God or say He does not exist will find out it's a terrible thing to fall into his judgment of the second death which will be eternal separation from God. God made us for His pleasure and gave humans the ability to procreate life. Anyone with a reasonable mind should realize we started with two people who were the first, and they did not come from evolution or from nothing. They came from one creator, who is the ultimate authority of the universe. Can a man make a house? Where do you think the ability came from? Can a man make a house if you put all the materials for building in a big pile and the man just looks at them, waiting for all of them to fly together in a unique way? That's what evolution says. I can assure you if a man could live 10,000 years just staring at the pile of materials God gave us to build a house with, he would see only erosion on the pile of materials. The erosion would not have happened if man had not fallen into disobedience to God in the beginning! All of nature is filled with entropy, and that is a result of the curse. The next world will not fade away and will be governed by the King of Glory. GOD IS!

If unbelievers keep trying to remove God from existence, they are bound by the devil's thinking! Truth is only known through Jesus Christ. Man is responsible for believing in our amazing God by looking at nature and all of the creativity I just talked about. (Romans 1: 18-21)

We make houses because the maker of man gave us the body, mind, heart, and creative ability to do it. His Spirit and His breath keeps all of us alive, and He knows the day of each person's first death because we all sin and do evil. He allows people to kill each other physically because He knows the spirit cannot be killed. Ref. (Matt 10:28)

He does not stop man from making evil choices, and man is responsible to not make them. The spirit of man will be judged, and he will be in one of two places forever. Heaven or Hades is real and waiting. I am writing all this hoping believers can show this portion to some people they would like to see saved. We are all a hybrid of good and bad, wonderful and corrupt. Is it not evident as we go through life? Tell everyone this is the way out; God is looking for everyone to admit they need His salvation and cry for mercy. He does not wish for any to perish. We have the option to turn to Him and cry for mercy. He knows the hearts that are sincere and longing for the everlasting life He has for all who come to Him. Eccl.3:11 tells us God has set eternity into people's hearts, and we all want to live forever.

God will reveal it to the people who seek Him. Come to the cross, for it is always a + Plus! God wants to add His eternity to your new life in Christ. There is no other way to be reconciled and live forever except through Jesus Christ. Since you are a Christian, accept the balance of being made in God's image in a wonderful way and the responsibility you have as a fallen creature to be grateful, accountable, and obedient to God. If you are struggling with your lower nature, be encouraged. God will finish what He started in you! (Philippians 1:6)

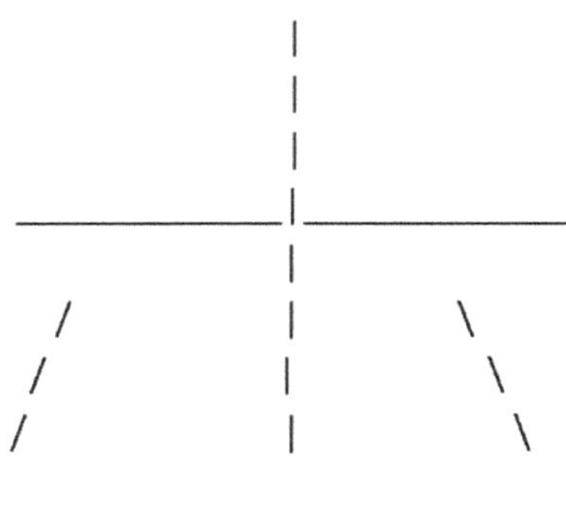

+

We are responsible persons who need to cry for mercy! Make your salvation a sure thing!

We are fallen creatures who need to cry for mercy! Make your salvation a sure thing!

+

We live by the Cross!
Our lives are centered
in the Christ of the Cross!
Live in balance by His Word!
May God have mercy on us all!

God's very big part shows us the extent of His loving Heart!

If I asked you what are the five principles of justification, what would your answer be? If I asked you what are the five principal expressions of saving faith, what would your answer be? I hope you enjoy this next topic. You can open your Bibles and go over these verses after I give them to you. The first principle of our justification is the Sovereign choice of God, out of love for all people, to offer salvation by His Grace in accordance with His Mercy. God chose to give us a way out of our horrible dilemma. Love turned His heart from His wrath against us, and He decided to carry out His costly plan to send Jesus. We are forever grateful. Romans 3:24, 1 Peter 2:10, and Hebrews 4:16 show us Mercy and Grace must go together.

From the kindness of God, we are justified by Mercy and Grace. The second principle of our justification is the Obedience of Jesus Christ, our Lord and Savior. It is His One Act of Righteousness which means His perfect, Holy life without sin. Romans 5:18-19, Hebrews 4:15, 2: Corinthians 5:21.

His perfection of character and loving behavior with no sin made Him the perfect sacrifice to pay for our sins. The third principle is His Shed Blood. The Crucifixion and atonement of the Lamb of God, Romans 5:9, 1 Peter 1:18-19.

The Blood of Jesus was necessary to atone for our sins! His death leads us to the fourth principle of our justification. Jesus Christ's Glorious Resurrection! Romans 4:25, 1 Corinthians 15:17, 20, Matthew 28:1-10 Up from the grave He Arose!

An important truth: Justification is not just-a-vacation-to-heaven. It is not for a temporary time of rest and enjoyment, and pleasure. It is an UNENDING ETERNAL REST WITH THE NOT GUILTY VERDICT FROM GOD, AND THE RICHES OF HIS GLORY IN CHRIST LAVISHED UPON ALL OF HIS JUSTIFIED CHILDREN FOREVER AND EVER WITHOUT END! AMEN! The resurrection was the last principle God carried out by Himself apart from any human involvement. The fifth principle of our justification is the one some of you may have answered right away when I asked the question. The fifth principle is The Correct Response to God! OUR FAITH! After you read the scriptures on the five principles, you will see they are in perfect order in, which came first to last. His loving Mercy and grace came first, then His perfect life without sin. Then His great suffering on the cross and then the Glory of His resurrection.

And finally, we came to the answer many of you knew immediately. Justified by Faith In Jesus Christ. This is the only one of the five that involved a small part from us, or it could not happen.

The verses I gave you confirm the principles, for they all tell us how we are justified using the word justification itself as the main topic of each verse. If we divide the percentages of the principles into five, because all five are necessary, we can say this fact. God performed 80 % of every person's salvation without any human action or participation. God wants to do more than 80%, and He can use people to get His percentage up from 80% to as much as 85%. Or maybe 90%, or what about 95%? I will attempt to explain this to all my precious brothers and sisters in Christ. God requires repentance from everyone to choose the option to get saved. If God did 100% of salvation, every person would come to Him, and no one would be lost.

This is not what the Bible says, and Jesus would have wasted His time as a man coming to earth and suffering. 100% would take away the response of repentance we all are required to do in humility and deep remorse with a contrite heart bowing down to Jesus. It comes down to dropping the poison of pride before God. It comes when we confess Jesus as God and confess our sins against Him. We must ask Him to save us and place our trust in Him to come into our life as Lord and Savior. So how much is the percentage of our involvement in the salvation process? The church says it is a mystery, and maybe it will remain one. You can't say 0%! This is a fact! Man's responsibility lies within the area of faith, which is a principle of 20% in the list of five necessary for justification.

We are all called to be ministers of reconciliation to bring the gospel to others. When Jesus ascended, He left us to do the greater things He told us to do when He went to the Father. Greater because He was limited to a body of flesh until He was glorified. We are many followers who He said would get the Holy Spirit to take the word of life to more people than He could reach in His limitations as a man. Taking it to the whole world is greater in quantity but never in quality! We have His Spirit.

When we obey the call to evangelize others, we find the ones who choose correct faith, the people who will receive the Lord by bowing down to God's offer and placing their trust in Jesus. I have experienced leading someone to the Lord, where the person got what seemed like 99% from God's part and only 1% of the response from the person. I experienced a miracle salvation with my mother that I share with others. Before I share, I can tell you that praying without ceasing can and will cause God to move on behalf of the lost ones being prayed for. It can take years but praying and loving people and building relationships by God's command to seek and save the lost will increase the number of salvations. In my case, I can say my mother was given a very small part of involvement in completing her salvation, and I will tell of how it was, and you can decide for yourself.

On the contrary, the small part of confessing you're a sinner and dropping your pride to say YES to God may seem to be a very big part for the person who is doing it! Remember, God has told Christians we are co-laborers to help His love reach the world. We are His servants of righteousness.

I prayed for my mother every day for 15 years to get saved. I served my mother with the labor of love many times, coming home from work. She lived between my job and my house. She had a stroke and was not supposed to live through the night. I had 50 men of God in the church praying for her. When the doctor came to me and told me the bad news he had, I said she was not ready to die. (I knew she was not on her way to the Lord.) He said, well, I know it's up to the man upstairs, but this is what's happening to her, and I got a complete diagnosis of her condition from him in 30 seconds. I said, by the way, Doctor, God is not a man you are! And now that you told me her condition I expect you to take care of her quickly, for she is in pain. The doctor started running to assist her and told the nurses to do the same thing. They jumped to care for her. He had told me to call the family to come right away. She probably won't make it through the night. She did not die and lived two more years. But she was still not ready to die until the four months before her time here on earth was going to end. Before my mother had the stroke, she was in a nursing home for three years for dementia, and I spent much time visiting her in the nursing home. I would sit by her bedside, holding her hand. I could not have a sensible conversation with her, saying little because of her dementia. After the stroke, she lost her speech completely, and she was shrinking away in her body. Mom can't talk anymore. My mom never accepted any verbal witness about God. I served her with deeds alone.

The pride was poison inside her. I always spend the whole morning in solitude with God, and one day I came to my feet quickly and looked upward, and I started praying as fervently as I could. I was hurting and was loud when I said, "I have been praying for her for 15 years and serving her without a word trying to love her into your salvation. Now she can't talk anymore. I almost yelled! You better save her! How can she pray with me or anyone when she can't make a verbal decision for You? She can't speak anymore! I was putting a demand on God, crying and wailing to Him, repeating these words: You better save her! You better save her!" Later I said I was sorry for talking to Him that way. Lord, I did not mean to be irreverent to you.

Two weeks later, on a Saturday morning, I felt strongly prompted to go and see her. I had never gone on Saturdays, and I knew God was tugging me to go. I walked into her room and sat down for a minute. I could feel the depth of the love of God permeating the room. I walked over to mom, looked into her eyes, and asked, "Are you ready to pray with me? She comprehended me and shook her head up and down with a yes answer. But she has not talked for two years? I said mom, repeat these words after me:

Dear Jesus (mom was able to repeat the words clearly), come into my heart. I believe you are God and that you died for me. I ask for your Holy Spirit and your salvation. I am sorry for my sins. She stared at me and stopped talking before the words I am sorry for my sins. I said, are you sorry for your sins? She stared at me without a word and with a confused look on her face. I bent down close to her, face to face, and said, mom, you have been holding out long enough. Are you sorry for your sins? Gazing at me, she said, I'm Sorry! I smiled, and she smiled back. When I left, I cried tears of joy for the privilege and the pleasure of watching God work a miracle of salvation. I knew for sure that the words, I am sorry for my sins, must come from the human agent, and God will never say them for us and do 100% to save someone. He gave her the ability to speak again after two years!

After that, my mother would smile when I entered her room, and we would rub noses like the Eskimos. She had a peaceful look on her face and smiled for four months before she died. The nursing home was a regular home with no religious connections, and no scriptures were hanging on the walls. I would have noticed, for I went there for five years. There were many pretty pictures and notes of information pinned up on the walls, but no scriptures. I went into the new room they brought her to about ten days before she died. I looked above her bed, and on the wall were gold letters with glitter like the ones you buy and peel off to stick on paper or a container or cabinet to identify something. It was confirmation that mom was going to be with God.

Matthew 19:26b was sticking on the wall with an exclamation point behind it. We all know it says that all things are possible with God! Evelyn, my mom's name was written under it! The gold letters were about an inch long and glittering with the truth. It was how my mother would have put it up if she could, and it certainly had a woman's touch. I marveled at the confirmation I was getting knowing there were no scriptures in this nursing home and no one was advocating it. I believe there are streets of gold described in Revelation that we will walk on in heaven or in the New Jerusalem.

Who put the gold letters up? Who could have known what happened unless my mom could speak to someone about her salvation? But mom never spoke for the last four months. She just smiled! She only spoke when we prayed! What about her name written after the scripture from Matthew? Someone knew her name, but who took the time to get them letters? I wondered why it was the only scripture I had ever seen in this home because

I looked at the walls of the rooms and went into many of them over the years, witnessing to people. Do you think there are some women angels? Regardless of gender, I think it could have been an Angel of God. 99% God and 1% Mom? I may find out later and when I get to heaven. I hope to recognize my mom again. But it won't be until I spend the equivalent of at least 10,000 years of our recorded time of duration on earth, staring into the Face of the Lord Jesus and bowing down to Him!

Part Two of God's very Big Heart!

[The Five saving expressions we all do when we get saved.]

We trust in God, which equals we believe in Him and obey Him when we get saved. We confess He is Lord with our mouth when we get saved. We repent with confession and the sorrow of a contrite heart for the sins we have committed against God, and we turn to Him. It's a turn-around event that equals the word Repent. We reach out for our salvation and take hold of it like a person grabbing the Jesus Saves Life Preserver- when we are drowning in our sin. We put it around the area of our heart under our arms to get pulled out of the troubled waters of sin. We receive Him into our hearts with open arms like He showed us on the cross. We open the door to our Divine guest and let Him in!

We Believe, Confess, Repent, Reach and Receive our salvation with these five expressions or actions of movement when we come to God. There are salvation scriptures for each of these expressions, and I will start with Believing in Jesus, which is placing your trust in Him alone to save you. John 3:16, John 3:36, John 6:40, Romans 10:9-10, Acts 16:31. These verses say Believe in Jesus, and you will be saved.

The next expression, Confessing Jesus is Lord, is found in Matthew 10:32, Hebrews 4:14, again Romans 10:9-10 to confess Him with our mouth as Lord, 1 John 4:15, 1 John 4:2.

The next expression is Repent, which confesses sin and sorrow, remorse and a humble, sincere brokenness of heart from sin. A changing of your mind and a 180-degree turn to God. Matthew 4:17, Acts 2:38, Acts 3:19, Acts 17:30. The next expression is Reach for it and take hold of it. Calling on the Lord is equal to reaching out to Him.

I called for Him, and He answered me. I reached Him for my salvation. I reached Him by my long-distance call to the throne of God! This one applies to me personally. Romans 10:8 NLT, Romans 10:13 calling him back. Acts 2:21, whoever calls on the name of the Lord shall be saved. Whoever means everyone who says, YES, I need God!

The last expression is to Receive Him. John 1:12, But as many as received Him, He gave them the right to become children of God, even those who believe in His name. Revelation 3:20 Behold I stand at the door and knock; if anyone hears My voice and opens the door, I will come into him or her and will dine with them, and he or she will dine with Me. John 17:8, read this verse in Jesus' prayer for all the believers in Him. We receive all His words. We answer when He calls and speaks to us with an open door from our hearts. The cross is always a plus+ Turn on Your B, C, R, R, R s!

```
                |
                |
                |
 _______________|_______________
                |
      /         |         \
     /          |          \
                |
```

God has five principles of Justification that He shows us in scripture. They come from His desire to save all people with His not guilty verdict!

+

We have five expressions of saving faith that cause us to come to God's loving salvation to receive the not guilty verdict. They are for all people. We believe, we we confess, we repent, we reach, and we receive Him into our hearts!

+

1. God's Mercy and Grace ------------He wants this for every person.
2. God's Righteousness-in exchange for our sin, the very Best Offer!
3. Jesus shed His Blood for us!--------- He died for us to live In Him!
4. His Resurrection! Eternal life for all who do the five expressions!
5. Faith! The correct response to God! Drop pride, Cry for Mercy!

Mercy and Grace--Titus 3:5
God's Righteousness----------------------------------2 Corinthians 5:21
The shed Blood of Jesus---------------------------------Romans 5:9
His Resurrection from the grave----------------------Romans 4:25
Faith, the Correct Response to God-------------------Romans 5:1

Here is another interesting Fact. The four main works of the Cross by God's loving action to save us and how much they might include our response actions. His Propitiation to deal with His wrath, He demonstrated all by Himself. We had no part in His choice to put all the wrath on Jesus. 25% of the work on the Cross is Propitiation. The removal of God's wrath against us for all our sins. Redemption is the Second main work of the cross.

Jesus' payment to Rescue us from the kidnapper, the evil one who stole our hearts through deception in Adam and Eve. Jesus paid the Ransom with His Blood. We had no part in this 25% of God's work. In Justification, we had at most a 5% part in the 25%. Reconciliation is the last main work that seals the forgiveness of God to us. It activates God's regeneration of the Spirit, and the Life of God now lives in an active relationship with believers. Reconciliation is an offshoot from Justification; 25% by God's doing. His part might be 95% up to 99% in God's four main works. >>>> God's huge part shows us the extent of His loving heart! (It's not 100 % from God!)

A Clear Look at what Hardens a Person's Heart

This attempts to bring the truth by defending God's love for all people. Some people think God hardened Pharaoh's heart as if it was unavoidable for Pharaoh. Some people think God caused this Pharaoh to be the bad guy created by God to give Israel misery and made him the villain in the deliverance story of Israel's escape from Egypt to the promised land. He was used by God but not created to be a lost man without a chance to know God. God knew his whole life and choices ahead of time. I know many Christians are aware of the chapters in Exodus and the verses where God speaks to Moses of hardening Pharaoh's heart. This is what Pharaoh said before God started all the consequences; Exodus 5:3, (Who is the Lord that I should obey His voice? I do not know the Lord and besides I will not let Israel go) In Exodus 4:21, The Lord said He would harden Pharaohs' heart. (Knowing Pharaoh's response ahead of time)

In 7:13, 7:22, 8:15, 8:19, and 8:33, Pharaoh's heart was hardened. In 9:34, it reads Pharaoh sinned and hardened his own heart. God does not make a person sin and never would be responsible for causing a person to sin. God can't sin, or He would stop being God. He is morally perfect in His Holiness. It is one of His eternal attributes. In verse 10:10, it says the Lord hardened Pharaoh's heart. What is going on is not hard to comprehend. Sin is the only thing hardening peoples' hearts. God is enforcing the consequences of sin, which increases the hardening the more it happens. Sin has the snowball effect. It gets bigger when you keep it rolling. God made men upright, but they have chosen sin and sought out many devices. God knows who will say yes to Him and who will come to Him in regard to the Old Testament promise or the New Testament appeal of Jesus Christ. We are all responsible to turn and seek God because His witness is plainly seen in creation. Ref. (Romans 1-18-23)

Pharaoh abused and brought cruelty to God's People for decades, and God knew ahead of time that this Pharaoh would not repent. If God says he will harden his heart, it is the consequence of the sin he keeps committing. Hebrews 3; 12-19 will confirm what sin does to our hearts. The topic of this section of scripture is the Peril of Unbelief. Unbelief is equal to disobedience, equal to sin, and equal to the hardness of heart. Verse 12, take care, brethren, that there not be in any one of you an evil, unbelieving heart that falls away from the living God. 13- But encourage one another daily, as long as it is still called today, so that none of you will be hardened by the deceitfulness of sin. Sin is the hardening factor, not God! Verse 15, Today, if you hear His voice, do not harden your hearts, as when they provoked Me.> (God)

Hebrews 3:18-19 says- And to whom did God swear that they would not enter His rest, but to those who were disobedient. So we see that they were not able to enter because of unbelief. We all discover that unbelief is really disobedience. We believe when we obey!

Pharaoh hardened his heart, and every time he said no to letting Israel go, his sin and hardness grew bigger. The consequences of sin result in a hard heart. Now we will see who can remove hardness and soften peoples' hearts. Who is the all-purpose heart softener? Ezekiel 36:25-27 reads-Then I (God) will sprinkle clean water on you and you will be clean, and I will cleanse you from all your filthiness (sins) and from all your idols. Moreover, I will give you a new heart and put a new spirit within you; and I will remove the heart of stone (hardness) from your flesh and give you a heart of flesh (one that's soft that I can work with.) And I will put my Spirit within you and cause you to walk in My statutes, and you will be careful to observe My ordinances. God is the all-purpose heart softener. The Holy Spirit works like a soft rain shower in people's hearts to bring growth. Just like the soft rain penetrates the ground to cause growth to the crops we need for food.

Psalm 65: 9-10, You (God) care for the land and water it; you enrich it abundantly. The streams of God are filled with water to provide the people with grain, for so you have ordained it. You drench the furrows and level its ridges. You, God, soften it with showers and bless its crops.) Have you ever experienced a drought when the ground gets so hard it starts to crack in many places? God wants to mend the hearts that crack from the hardness of sin with the Living Waters of Jesus Christ. He wants to gently penetrate your hardness of heart. Our potter can work with the clay when it is soft. He will make it soft and then work His will out for us! God would have wanted even Pharaoh to know Him and worship Him, but Pharaoh chose to run his own life. He was held responsible, like all men, to see God in creation and not suppress the truth of God for a lie. God is a perfect Judge, and no one can tell me that God does not love all sinners and desire salvation for them. Pharaoh had a chance to repent after seeing the miracles of God but refused because he followed Satan rather than God. He loved the darkness rather than the light. Our view of sin and the hardness of the heart is in balance when we know the attributes of our eternal God, whose eyes can observe a person's whole life ahead of time! He can predict every choice a person will make! Be glad you know our amazing God and that we will receive the inheritance of heaven because of the Love of Jesus Christ in our lives! + We said Yes to Christ!

Mercy and Grace
+
Justice and Righteousness

We will focus on another area of God's heart and mind for exercising His Justice and righteousness to deal with the transgressions against Him. When people do not heed the warnings that justice serves, the next step after the warning would be rendering the due penalty for all nonconformity to God's moral righteousness. Justice always deals with warnings and penalties. The ones who do justice carry out God's plan to bring His righteousness in place of unrighteousness. It comes down to the fact that God wants Christians to exercise love and mercy from His mind and heart and justice and righteousness from His mind and heart also. There are many scriptures to put on both sides of the cross with this integration of God's attributes. There are two strong Proverbs to speak loudly about the justice and righteousness side.

Prov. 21:3-To do righteousness, and justice is desired by the Lord rather than sacrifice.

Proverbs 21:15-The execution of justice is joy for the righteous, but it is terror to the workers of iniquity.

Micah 6:8 is an absolute verse for all Christians to heed. He (God) has told you, O man, what is good and what does the Lord require of you but to do justice, to love mercy, and to walk humbly with your God? This integrates the justice, mercy, and submission God wants to see actively present in our lives. We know and understand clearly these attributes which God shares with us. The righteousness of Jesus from 2nd Corinthians 5:21 is the moral Holiness of God. Justice always deals with all nonconformity to Christ's righteousness or the moral Holiness of God. Mercy is sometimes compared to God's kindness. If I were to ask my brothers and sisters in Christ are you striving to participate in showing mercy and kindness along with doing justice, what would you say? I can tell you that in all my time as a Christian, I am short on the justice side. Nevertheless, God wants a balance here.

The justice scriptures are Matthew 23:23, 2 Corinthians 7:11 NIV, Proverbs 21:3, 21:15, Micah 6:8, Isiah 56:1, proverbs 24:25, 27:5, Matthew 12:18-20. Listen to these verses. Jesus was fulfilling the scripture from Isiah 42:1-3 BEHOLD MY SERVANT WHOM I HAVE CHOSEN; MY BELOVED IN WHOM MY SOUL IS WELL-

PLEASED; I WILL PUT MY SPIRIT UPON HIM, AND HE SHALL PROCLAIM JUSTICE TO THE GENTILES. HE WILL NOT QUARREL NOR CRY OUT, NOR WILL ANYONE HEAR HIS VOICE IN THE STREETS. A BATTERED REED HE WILL NOT BREAK OFF, AND A SMOLDERING WICK HE WILL NOT PUT OUT UNTIL HE LEADS JUSTICE TO VICTORY. It is written in all capitals and is supposed to capture our hearts and minds for that reason. The scriptures on mercy and kindness (all part of love) are Matthew 5:7, Lamentations 3:22-23 Titus 3:4-5, Luke 18:11-14, Ephesians 4:32, Psalm 57:1, Psalm 6:2, and listen to James 2:13- For judgment will be merciless to the one who has shown no mercy; mercy triumphs over judgment. 1 Peter 2:10, it is very clear here, capitals again, for you once were NOT A PEOPLE, BUT NOW YOU ARE THE PEOPLE OF GOD; you had NOT RECEIVED MERCY, but now you have RECEIVED MERCY. It is a matter of life and death to some people. Lord, help us be doers of justice and be merciful and kind to others showing God's love and what He requires from His people to make Jesus known to all.

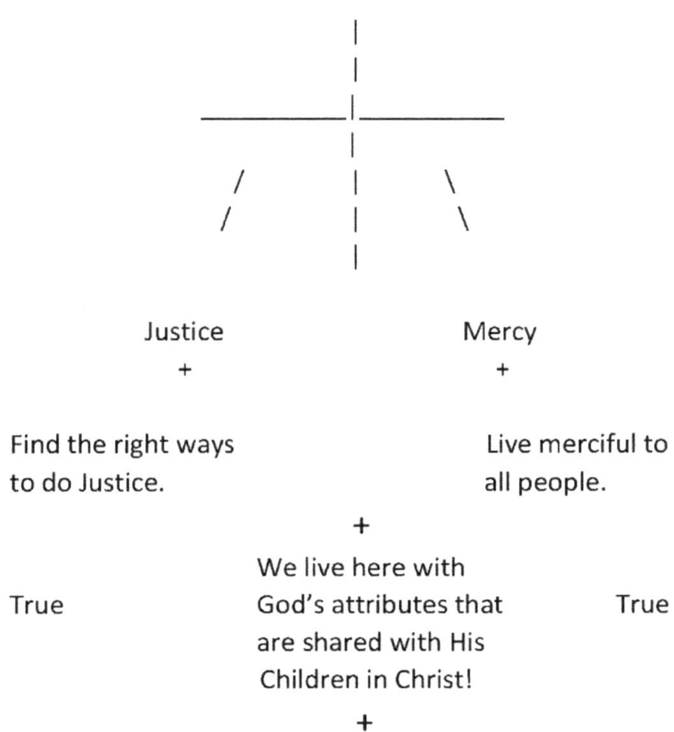

There is a reason why many of us fail to balance these two communicable attributes God gives to us. We experienced great mercy when we were saved. At first, we may not have realized how God bypassed our judgment of eternal separation from Him. We could only think of His amazing mercy and love and not how Jesus became the substitute for being executed for all the injustice that will occur until He returns. It is also not easy to fight injustice unless it is done without Christians blowing up the abortion clinics and calling down fire on all the evildoers. All of us as Christians are still waiting for the injustice to be gone in reality, and we live in it every day. We often have it happen to us. We say it will not leave till Jesus comes back. Luke 18: 7-8 says- Now shall not God bring about justice for His elect, who cry to Him day and night, and will He delay long over them? I tell you He will bring justice speedily, but when the Son of man returns, will He find faith on earth? Are we praying for the doers of evil? Loving our enemies? Faith works through love! Faith would like to thrive! God loves His human enemies. PRAY with persistence day and night so mercy will triumph over judgment!

The Power of God's Holiness Unique and One of a Kind!

We will observe God's supernatural power with His total Holiness. God has allowed us to share in His moral holiness, which is transitive to us by His grace when we are saved. But there is also the uniqueness of God's Holiness, where He is set high above everything in the universe. His attribute, which the Holy Trinity only shares, is because of the personhood of God. The power to call all creation into being and control the universe is God's and His alone. The power of love, life, light, and the authority that commands everything to be or not to be is His alone. The resurrection power to raise the dead by His Holiness is what we will focus on, and we will discover more about our amazing God.

Romans 1:1-5 will be the verses we will look at to gain insight. You will see the Metaphysical, Unique God who is not like any other, demonstrating His power and great love in the resurrection of Jesus. Showing proof of His ultimate authority by the power of the resurrection. After Paul greets the Romans in his writing and tells them he is set apart for the gospel of God, he directly moves to who it's about. He starts to explain the Son of God to them. Verse 3, and concerning His Son, who was born of a descendant of David according to the flesh, who was declared the Son of God with power by the resurrection from the dead, according to the Spirit of holiness, Jesus Christ our Lord. There are two distinct ways to describe God's holiness. He is separated from His creatures and creation and exalted in infinite majesty, the relation of the infinite to the finite. This aspect is God's metaphysical one, where He stands alone far beyond all other things created. He is One of a kind and the one from which all other things came into being. God is the ruler of the universe. God has made the earth and come to earth and proven this fact through Jesus Christ. Man's greatest endeavor should be to know God and not to venture past our limitations by searching the universe for other life or places to live. God's unique holiness is something we can never share, and it is good that we can't. He is where all our security and eternal life exist. We can receive eternal life in Christ, and we do not have to gain comprehension of every wonderful fact and the knowledge we can't possess. Love will surpass all knowledge, and glory is forever with God. He is UNIQUE, and He is the resurrection and the life.

John 11: 25-26 may be the most powerful verses in the bible. They are certainly the most encouraging ones. There is no resurrection without the Spirit of God's holiness. The moral perfection and the cosmic power of the eternal God combined in the resurrection of Jesus. All three persons of the Trinity were involved in the resurrection by the essence of God in which they are equal. We will start with Jesus taking His part in His resurrection.

John 10:17-18 will surely open the ears and eyes of our hearts as we read this scripture! For this reason, the Father loves Me because I lay down My life so that I may take it up again. No one has taken it away from Me, but I lay it down on My initiative, I have the authority to lay it down, and I have the authority to take it up again. This commandment I received from My Father. John 6:40, For this is the will of My Father, that everyone who beholds the Son and believes in Him, may have eternal life; and I (Jesus) will raise him up on the last day. Now we will look at the Fathers' part in the resurrection of Jesus. Peter is preaching with power as the church is expanding after Pentecost.

Acts 2:23-24, this man, delivered by the predetermined plan of God, you nailed to a cross by the hands of godless men and put Him to death. And God raised Him up again, ending the agony of death since it was impossible for Him to be held in its power. 1 Corinthians 6:14, Now God has not only raised the Lord but will also raise us up through His power. Now we will look at the Holy Spirit's contribution to the resurrection of Jesus. Romans 8:11, But if the Spirit (Holy Spirit) of Him who raised Jesus from the dead dwells in you, He who raised Christ Jesus from the dead will also give life to your mortal bodies through His Spirit (Holy Spirit) who indwells you. We thank you, Dear Holy Spirit, for your part in raising Jesus from the dead and for being a member of the Cosmic Threesome that is metaphysically above and beyond all of creation. You are Unique in the majesty of your holiness! As Christians with the best possible promise in the universe, we must relinquish our lives to the control of the Holy Spirit. Romans 8:14 says those who the Spirit of God is leading are sons and daughters of God. We are to walk according to the Spirit and not the flesh nature, in keeping with Him step by step until we fly to glory! Can you imagine your resurrection or the ascension of the saints in the Rapture? It will be an incredible and magnificent experience!

The Deepest Intimacy with God!

We will see just how intimate God wants to be with us, and you may be surprised because of how extreme it is. The balance of love is more love, and love to God moves to an extreme level without compromise. There is no balance between love and hate or love and fear. There is no balance between Humility and the pride of the flesh or between God's wisdom and man's finite intelligence. When love from God and to God is extreme, the rest of life will come into balance! It's the only place to be extreme. It's the only thing to grasp with your heart, soul, and mind and never let go of. It is the only place where more and more is never too much and where we find who we are in God. There's freedom and peace that goes past our comprehension. Besides being extreme, unless God's love comes into a person's life, they will be separated from Him forever. His love is crucial. His love is what every person is searching for in all the secondary things they take part in. It is eternal over the temporal and the infinite over the finite. He put eternity into the hearts of men and women and wants us to be redeemed to that eternity. He wants to remove the body of sin in our first death and raise us up with the glory of a resurrection body in the image of His Son, Jesus our Lord. Is God Intimate? There's no question about it! We will examine the scriptures where He wants to give us His love.

Let's start with Hosea 11:3-4. God will take us in His arms and He will teach us how to walk. He wants to heal us and lead us with bonds of love. He wants to lift our heavy burdens. He will bend down to feed us. He wants an intimate relationship with His people. In Isiah 42:6, God wants to hold us by the hand, for He is our loving Father. Let's look at Psalm 27:8 and Psalm 105:4. God wants us to seek His face continually. Look at Deuteronomy 33:26-27 God rides the Heavens to our help, and underneath are His everlasting arms! There is no end to the extent of help God can show us, and we can know His everlasting arms are holding us. Revelation 3:20 is real. He is knocking on the door of our hearts to sit with us face to face. Here is a poem about how intimate our Heavenly Father wants to be with us. It focuses on the Father's love for all His children. Before I share the poem, you have to envision the details as I explain them to you. Picture this in your mind and feel it in your heart. God, the Father, wants to take us through the festival of abundant life because we are in His Son, Jesus Christ. God, the Father, has a big roll of two-part tickets in one of His hands. His other hand is holding you and me by the hand. Imagine this and ask God to help you because it's true! We are at the festival, and God is next to us, going through it with every step we take. We have a loving Father that will not let go of each one of us. The two-part tickets represent God's blessings and plans for our life. He wants to give the tickets to us one by one as we walk with Him. God has a perfect time to share His blessings and plans with us as our relationship grows in oneness with Him. He takes His part in enjoying each one of the tickets with us. He is the giver of all good things, and that is His wonderful nature. He knows how to nourish His children and lead them with His perfect timing. He wants us to seek His face and ask for continuing instructions and guidance. He wants to share everything with us, including His Holy discipline and all blessings. We have received the moral Holiness of God, which is the righteousness of Jesus our Lord. We will grow in the righteousness of Jesus by the Spirits' sanctification.

We must keep our eyes on God's face and not focus too much on the roll of tickets representing God's provision for us. A problem develops when we take our eyes off His face and are more concerned with what He will do for us or give us next. The focus on His hand over the focus on His face can lead to compromise and even idolatry. Will you tell me if you have ever been in this situation or if you are in it right now? It's time for the poem, and I hope you enjoy it and, perhaps, learn from it-------The Festival of Abundant Life with God-------Festival, Festival, Fun, Fun, Fun! We're grabbing God's tickets, and we're starting to run! Leaving Father behind thinking, Oh, He won't mind if I focus entirely on me, myself, and I!

For the tickets I took are His blessings and plans; they're God-oriented, but they're now in my hands. Is there anything wrong with me taking control of the blessings and plans my Father wants to bestow? Hey! Wait just a minute. There's no way this will work. What about our relationship? Maybe He's hurt? With my eyes on His tickets instead of His face, forgive me, dear Father, for my selfish, frantic pace! Bring me back to the right focus, dear Father of grace, with my eyes off your tickets, seeing only your face. But some of you say I was only standing on the promises of God! That is okay, but it's all about your focus; are you staying focused on His face and walking at His pace? Are you receiving from His hand at the time that He has planned? It's only then you can say; I have learned where to focus, dear Father of grace. My eyes are now off your tickets; they're on only your face! I share all your blessings each day, one by one. The festival's great because You get everything done! Each ticket You give me is the joy of your heart; it helps our relationship take a new part. Down the pathway to glory toward the fullness of light, one step at a time, You make another thing right. Father, give me love with your patience and help me walk the right pace; for I live with my Savior seeking only your face! Child of God: maintain intimacy with the Father, the giver of all good things. Enjoy Him and worship

Him. He is your greatest blessing, above and beyond all the secondary blessings He can give us. Obey Him!

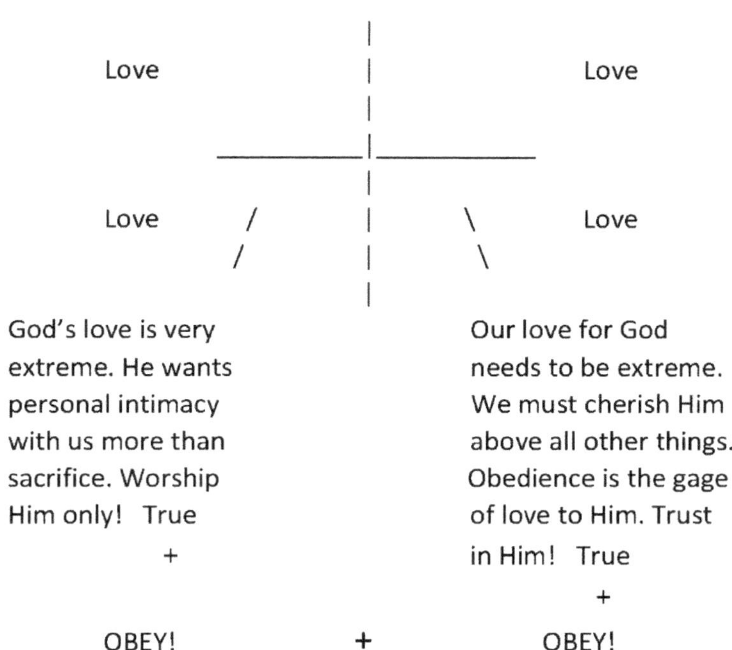

Live with God's love always!
The balance of love is more love!
We owe love to God and all people.
We are in love debt forever and love
payments will never stop! Romans 13:8

This is a list of Blessings that are on Gods' Roll of tickets for all His Children-- His provision to us in our life- The breath of life by His Spirit that He gives to all people every day they live here on earth-- Food and shelter, water, clothing-- Critical relationships with family and friends, Wife, husband, children, and grandchildren, best friends we have in life-- Wisdom, intelligence, and creative ability to build and manage things in life-- Work to earn our wages to meet all our physical needs-- House and car and pets that we love-- Special gifts to the body of Christ to be employed to build Gods' Kingdom--

Discipline to conform us to the image of Christ-- Trials and testing to produce the character of love to others-- All the good parts of technology with a boundary God would want to keep us from forgetting Him-- The correct portion of responsibility at the right time to receive it-- A servant's heart to others and a heart of humility, honor and gratitude for God-- The fruit of the Spirit in our lives-- Healing in our bodies when we are sick and doctors to help us get well-- A good mind to discover life and live it sensibly-- A healthy soul that is satisfied with contentment and peace to all who trust in Him-- The beauty of His creation even in its fallen state--The freedom to choose and contribute to the world we live in-- Give thanks every day for all God's provision and most of all for Knowing Him and His love forever, Amen!

The Ticket to admit one or the two part tickets God has?

It's our Choice as His Children!

Admit one only
Self-Centered
No Intimacy
x

Focus on the Tickets x

God's Part
His Giving He enjoys
each day!
....
Our part of God's
Blessing to us!

Focus on His face! +

Keeping our eyes on God's face means our love for Him is the constant reciprocal love out of humility, honor, and gratitude for Who He is. It brings us beyond, and above all, He can give us in the provision we need for our physical lives and empowers our soul and Spirit. His hand will never be short when we focus on His face. The child who grabs His two-part tickets and lets go of His hand will see the tickets are going to admit one only. This will leave the child feeling empty inside from not walking with God. Self-centeredness will never satisfy because of a frantic pace from an unwillingness to wait for God's timing. His love is patient for a very good reason. He knows pride and impatience leads to potential destruction. (Eccl. 7:8)

Realize the poem is the truth, for God so loved us that He died in our place to reconcile us into the deepest relationship possible, and it is for all eternity! Freedom is putting God, Jesus, and the Holy Spirit over everything. God always looks at us with a half of a smile on His face, all the time, and it is a smile of approval because of who we have become in Jesus Christ! Allow Him to enjoy all of the good things He will do for all of us who completely trust in Him. He is our life and breath, and the words of Jesus were repeated in Acts 20:35b (it is better to give than to receive) God is the Better One! Allow Him to enjoy His giving to us! It really does go this deep! Amen!

Wisdom is much more than making wise Choices

God's wisdom is in His character, and we see it all in Christ alone!

I was told a definition of wisdom when I was a new Christian that sounded appropriate, but as I grew and searched the scripture, I saw wisdom is much more than discernment of making wise choices. Like the fruit of the Spirit, which are all qualities of God's character, wisdom from above is also a list of God's character qualities. Walking by the Spirit and walking in God's wisdom are very closely related. Solomon asked for wisdom in 1 Kings 3:6-9, and God gave it to Him, but Solomon was deceived by wives he took who worshipped foreign gods, and He fell into idolatry. Solomon's wisdom was discernment without the steady character qualities of real wisdom from above. We are blessed to know that in Christ, we have been given access to His wisdom, which is much more complete than Solomon's. Who could be a godly husband to more than one woman and have many concubines simultaneously? A close look at David and Solomon's life could only encourage us to know Jesus much deeper and rely on Him as the perfect role model for any man or woman to follow or exalt. For He alone is God! A man or woman after God's heart should also be a man or woman after God's wisdom in Christ alone. The fruit and the treasure of wisdom is in Jesus Christ himself. The wisdom from above is described in James 3:17. The wisdom from above is first pure, then peaceable, gentle, reasonable, full of mercy and good fruits, unwavering, without hypocrisy. 1 Corinthians 1:30 tells us--By God's doing, we are in Christ Jesus who became to us wisdom from God and righteousness and sanctification and redemption. Colossians 2:2-3 tells all of us that we can attain the wealth that comes from the full assurance of understanding in a true knowledge of God's mystery, that is, Christ Himself, in whom are hidden all the treasures of wisdom and knowledge. Divine wisdom and knowledge live in us as spirit-filled Christians, with the love of the Holy Spirit poured into our hearts. So God wants us to walk in the fruit of the Holy Spirit in Galatians 5:22-23. The fruit of the Spirit is love, joy, peace, patience, kindness, goodness, faithfulness, gentleness, and self-control, against such things, there is no law. The fruit is directly from the lawgiver, who can only be God. The lawgiver is above the law. We can walk in the wisdom of God and in the fruit of the Spirit if we do not walk according to the flesh but according to the Spirit. (Romans 8:4) God has enabled us to fulfill the requirements of His law of the Spirit. What this all comes to is something we all have heard more than once. Our flesh nature cannot walk in the wisdom of God, and we can't be fruit bearers apart from God. It is a never-ending desire for the Life and love of God to live freely in us. He is the Vine, and we are the branches. We do want the fruits of wisdom from above and to walk by the Spirit and produce the fruit of the Spirit. There is a proverb that lets us know how we can do better in living in God's wisdom. Proverbs 17:24 says, wisdom is in the presence of one who has understanding, but the eyes of a fool are on the ends of the earth. We had a close look at the word understanding in previous teachings. We set our minds on things above and do our best not to focus on this temporary world that will pass away from all of us. Standing under God and obeying His word will give us all the wisdom we need in this life. Try not to get caught in the culture that sees only the present life here on earth. This is hard for all of us, but we are living with Christ in us, and Eternal life is present. He is wisdom and love and has the character we are being conformed to by the Spirit's sanctification. To die daily to the flesh that Paul speaks about is complete submission to the Spirit. This is the way of the Christian life. Give yourself to God daily in real submission, and watch what an amazing privilege and pleasure it is to watch Him work His will through you. He is all we need! Faith would always be the correct response to God, and this response to yield our lives into His control is what He wants most. It shows His glory to others through you and me and lets us see life indeed! All of life is in the treasure of wisdom and knowledge and the fullness of love in the Holy Spirit. In Jesus, we have everything. We can claim as Christians that we are a person who knows it all! I went up to a fine man I knew that was a Pastor at a very good church when I lived in the northwest suburbs of Chicago. He had just finished his message. I said to our Pastor Wayne, I think you're a know it all! He had a strange look on his face, but before it could droop, I said you really know Jesus well, and Jesus knows everything; that makes you a know it all! I knew him well enough to get away with that. He was one of my teachers in Bible College.

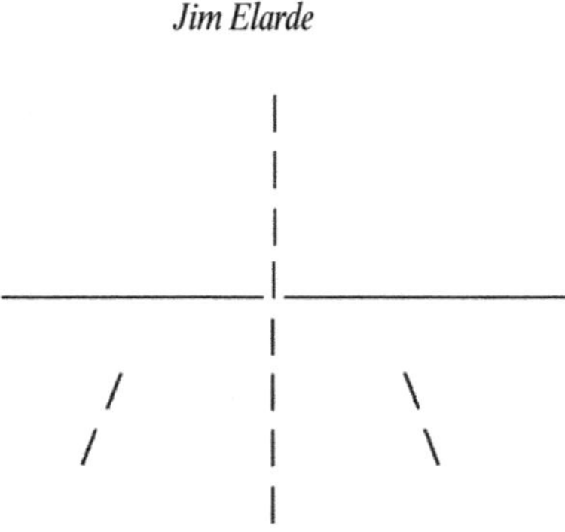

Wisdom is Love from God's character.		Wisdom from God is in His character.
True	+	True

Wisdom is part of God's Love and controls His perfect Character! Walk in the wisdom from above! The treasure of wisdom is in Jesus Christ! 1 Corinthians 1:30, Colossians 2: 2-3

Section Two

God's Creative Communication

Bible Versions for Section Two are NIV, NASB, and NLT, designated with each full verse written out. There is one verse from the Message Bible, and it is designated. Ref. means reference that applies to all Bible translations to support the principles being discussed.

Section Two: Creative Communication to teach God's Word without losing a Balance of Truth. Inspiration with God's illumination as He speaks His Word in a unique and different way!

The Great Breaker and Trainer!

Psalm 32: 9-11 NASB version- Do not be like the horse or mule, which have no understanding but must be controlled by bit and bridle, or they will not come to you. Many are the woes of the wicked, but the Lord's unfailing love surrounds the man who trusts in Him. Rejoice in the Lord and be glad you righteous; sing, all you who are upright in heart!

People are born with a flesh nature that is stubborn, self-centered, wild, and destructive. In many ways, we are like wild horses. God has just related the nature of man with that of an unruly horse or mule in the metaphor in this Psalm.

Question: how can God deal with a stubborn and wild creature without forcing control? God does not want to use the bit and bridle, but He has to use a rope of discipline! It's time to use our imagination. Picture God as the Great Breaker and Trainer of wild horses. Picture God pursuing the wild horses. He knows their value and has the knowledge, love, and patience to make something beautiful and wonderful out of all of them. Unfortunately, some of them will never cooperate with the breaking process. There are many valleys full of wild horses. Many are sought, but few are caught. There is a whole cast of characters in this story and two places where the horses can be. I will share the cast of characters before we get into the details of God's pursuit.

1. The Great Breaker and Trainer is God
2. The new baby Christian horse will be the one God catches for this story.
3. The excellent performing horse is the one God has trained well.
4. The visiting fellow horse is a counselor and a friend.
5. The mountain lion is Satan
6. The wild filly is a seductive tool of Satan
7. The Angels are God's loyal guards
8. The preacher in the story is me; the inspired writer by God's Grace.
9. The wild life is the first place the horses are found in darkness and fear.

10. The Great Breaker and Trainers Corral is the second place the horses can be. It is much better in the long run for them to find it; Love and eternal life forever!

We find that wild horses are often kicking at each other and knocking their heads together. They often try to overpower one another. God, as our Great Breaker and Trainer, is trying to stop them from kicking, banging, and acting in a violent and fearful manner. He wants to save them from themselves. God has a great lasso that He is twirling with His mighty right arm. His arm can stretch and throw the lasso as far as He wants to. The lasso represents His saving power which comes in the gospel message. We know God offers salvation through Jesus Christ. Our Great Breaker and Trainer throws the lasso around the lowest part of a wild one's neck and tightens it firmly. What He is really after is the heart. He intends to give all of them a home in His Great Corral. He intends to break them from their unruly ways and train them to be prize show horses for His glory! The ones who are not caught will end up with the bit and bridle of the devil, who will keep them in fear and lead them to destruction.

If God doesn't rescue them, they face a certain death, and they will never know God's love for them. When our great Breaker and Trainer's rope lands around one of the wild ones, and that wild one is reeled into the corral, we will have a new baby Christian horse. Some of the wild ones will run and jump even more when they see the rope around the neck of the horse next to them. They are rejecting the change that is about to take place. When God pulls a new baby in, they come into a place where there is a new and abundant life. They will be surrounded by love and freedom. God keeps throwing His rope in every direction, hoping to catch all the wild ones, but some of them will dodge the rope forever. Some of them seem to like being completely out of control. As our Great Breaker and Trainer looks at every new horse he has caught, he says; I will do my best to make this one a prize show horse for my glory! It will be a delight to train each one of them.

When a new baby is caught, he will still show a bit of resistance because he has a rope around his neck. He was free to roam wherever and whenever without a boundary in the wild life. When a new baby starts to resist the rope, God says stop fighting me; you are a stubborn and self-centered creature. If you knew my intentions and what I could do with your life, you will learn to submit to the discipline. You don't realize what I can do through you and how I can work in you. You were heading for destruction and unable to change your destructive ways by yourself. Now let's look at the new baby and all the changes that will take place for one who just got caught. He has been pulled into the corral, and the rope that is around his neck extends to every point in the corral. It does not permit the new baby to get past the circular fence of our Great Breaker and Trainers protection.

Each baby is brought to the center of the corral because that is the safest place to be. Before a new baby is about to start his training, he feels a deep peace come over him. He feels a new security, and he slows down to take a good look at everything in the corral. He feels a deep change has taken place inside of him. He sees a huge water trough made of gold. It is filled with pure water, and there is a pipeline of water flowing to it to keep it filled constantly. The other horses are drinking, and it keeps being refilled. There are huge hay stacks soaked with milk, honey, and huge bags of horse feed with a horse's favorite food. Food is abundant all around, and many horses give their food to each other and rub their necks together. He senses that someone has cared so much for him and the other horses that they are allowed to eat and drink freely. He does not have to look for his food anymore. He has stopped searching and knows he has more than enough in supply. This new baby is grateful and looks toward our Great Breaker and Trainer, who pulled him to safety in the corral. He is now very curious about his new home and wants to discover more. It seems too good to be true. With God, everything is good because it is true! Our Great Breaker and Trainer is going to start His masterful work. He will change His new possession into a prized performer for His glory to be revealed. A problem develops when the new baby feels the rope tighten around his neck. It was loose with no pressure, but now he feels some pressure. He says I have much comfort and I'm eating and drinking freely.

I have much peace and love, but now I am getting squeezed by the pressure of this rope. It's our Great Breaker and Trainer doing it. Why is He interrupting my new comfort zone? He is trying to pull me closer to himself. How much can I trust Him? After all, he still has a rope around my neck! I don't trust Him enough, so I will keep my distance from Him for a while. I want to be completely comfortable with my new home. I don't want any unnecessary pressure! Hey! I can't get away from Him! God is starting to apply some pressure. I feel it inside of me. He doesn't want to let me go.

(The Preacher enters in) Philippians 1:6 NASB He who began a good work in you will perfect it until the day of Christ Jesus.

(Meanwhile, back at the corral) The new baby is saying to himself; maybe if I resist Him enough, He will let me go for a while and ease the pressure of the rope. So, God realizes the stubborn nature of the new baby and that he won't submit to the rope of discipline for training. God does not want to use the bit and bridle. He wants willing cooperation. He lets the rope out for the new baby giving him plenty of slack. The new baby can run with a loose rope, but it will only be temporary. I'm glad He is giving me some slack, says the new baby. I feel like running again! I am very familiar with running. Why should I get used to just walking gracefully? The baby starts to run from the center of the corral. Ouch! I smashed my head against a post at the end of the corral! My neck is burning from the rope because I used up all the slack when the rope stopped me from going over the edge of the corral. I ran too close to the edge! My neck burns, and my head is injured. I feel like I did when I was in the wild life, bumping heads with the other wild ones and fighting all the time. I need healing, and I need loving care. Maybe I should not have resisted our Great Breaker and Trainer? But what right does He have to control me?

(The preacher enters in) 2 Corinthians 5:15, Christ died for all so that they who live might no longer live for themselves, but for Him who died and rose again on their behalf. Romans 12:1-2, present yourself to the Lord in worship and be transformed with a new mind to do God's will.

(Meanwhile, back at the corral) The new baby is lying on the ground and suffering burns and bruises. He is thinking maybe our Great Breaker and Trainer will overlook the fact that I resisted Him and help me. His thinking was right.

(The preacher enters in) Lamentations 3: 22-23, NIV. Because of the Lord's great love, we are not consumed, for His compassions never fail. They are new every morning. Great is His faithfulness.

2 Timothy 2:13 If we are faithless, He remains faithful; for He cannot deny Himself.

(Meanwhile, back at the corral) Very calmly, a gentle hand starts rubbing a soothing ointment all over the burns on the new baby's neck. A gentle hand starts to caress his aching head, and he feels healing almost instantly. He gets well and comes back to the center of the corral. Good health is compatible with the center of the corral! The new baby begins to eat and drink freely once again. His peace and joy have returned because of the healing, compassion, and mercy that was shown. After several days the new baby feels the rope tighten around his neck again. He starts to think, what should I do? The last time I ran away, I got burned and bruised. God seems to be waiting for me to respond to His rope. He is tugging gently. He is gentle and patient and not harsh or in a hurry. Maybe I will walk with Him and see what He wants to do with me with His rope around my neck. I am going to keep a little distance with just a little bit of slack in the rope. I don't want to get too close too soon. I don't know how much I can trust Him. He has given me a new home with plenty of loving care. I'm eating and drinking freely without searching, but He still has a rope around my neck. I wonder why He wants to control me.

(The preacher enters in) Ref. Proverbs 14:12 and 16:25 (Created paraphrase) There is a way that seems right to a horse, but its end is a bottle of glue or a bar of soap. Psalm

33:17 NASB. A horse is a false hope for victory, nor does it deliver anyone by its great strength.

(Meanwhile, back at the corral) The new baby says I will cooperate with our Great Breaker and Trainer. After all He has done for me, He deserves my trust. I will give Him the benefit of my doubt. Suddenly, the new baby turns to the right and sees a horse he knew in the wild life. It was one he hung around with and remembered when the horse left the herd one day. He was rescued by God before the new baby was. The new baby is watching his former friend walk gracefully and prance about in a way he never saw any other horse do. He sees him hurdle over obstacles and performs with confidence and great skill. He observes very closely as this horse performs without the rope around his neck. Our Great Breaker and trainer has released this horse to perform in the most excellent manner. The new baby thinks of how this horse was when he was with him in the wild life. He was stumbling and complaining and always running away from the mountain lion trying to attack the herd looking for horse meat. The new baby realizes there are no mountain lions near the corral and that the center of the corral is the safest place in the new life he is now living. He remembers that there was always the possibility of the mountain lion attacking one of them when they were in the wild life. As he continues to watch the excellent performing horse, he wonders if God can show him how to perform in an excellent way and teach him skills beyond his own capabilities. He wonders if he could prance so gracefully and hurdle over obstacles also. No, I could never do these things, He said to himself. One of the obstacles his former buddy jumped over was at least Six feet high! I would probably break my legs. But wait a minute. In the wild, this excellent performing horse was the weakest one in the herd. Then, the new baby said he was never afraid of the mountain lion like his weaker buddy was. He believed the mountain lion would not mess with him knowing he was stronger than his buddy. He was the bravest horse in the herd. He looks over and sees his buddy, the excellent performer stopping, and two of God's helpers are putting the obstacle bar much higher. They are setting the bar on fire. The excellent performer is bowing down to our Great Breaker and Trainer. His lips are moving, and he is making sounds that are difficult to interpret. The excellent performer is standing on his back legs with his front legs held high, giving praise to our Great Breaker and Trainer.

(The preacher enters in) 1 Thessalonians 5: 16-17 NIV. Be joyful always. Pray continually.

(Meanwhile, back at the corral) The performing horse is getting ready to attempt to leap over the high bar with fire burning on the top of it. The new baby thinks he will never make the jump, for a horse is too heavy to do such a jump. Where did the excellent performer get this kind of courage? He has started his run and is going full speed toward the bar. Wow! He cleared the bar by three feet, over the fire, and landed perfectly. He jumped higher than the Bull from Chicago! Number 23! He is bowing down to God again, and he is thanking Him for what had to be supernatural power. How are these things possible?

(The preacher enters in) Matthew 19:26b With God, all things are possible. Jeremiah 32:27- I am the God of all flesh. Is there anything too hard for me? Philippians 4:13 implies we can do many difficult things through Christ, who strengthens us. (Meanwhile, back to the corral) After seeing his friend perform incredible things, the new baby Christian horse says, I want our Great Breaker and Trainer to do something wonderful in my life. Then he said something he should not have said. I can do better things than this buddy of mine from the wild life. I was always better than him at everything in our herd. I was stronger, faster, and not nearly as wimpy and fearful. The mountain lion stayed away from me and went after the weaker ones. Hey! The rope is tugging me, and our Great Breaker and Trainer will start training one of His very best. It's my turn, and I am ready! I want greater things from Him than I just saw from my old friend. I will show Him and the other horses in the corral what great really is!

(The preacher enters in) Trouble is coming with a capital T. James 4:6b NASB. God is opposed to the proud but gives grace to the humble. Proverbs 16:5a NIV. The Lord detests the proud of heart.

(Meanwhile, back at the corral) God has heard the words of the new baby. He squeezes the rope on the new baby's neck and pulls the rope with a surge of power. Bang! Crash! Boom! The baby is on his belly, with his face getting dragged through the dirt. The rope comes off of him, and our Great Breaker and Trainer throws it around another horse's neck. What happened, said the new baby? How can He do this to me? Why isn't He working with me? I want to be a Super Star Stud! At this time, another fellow horse who the baby had never met before comes prancing over to check things out. The visiting fellow horse says I see you're on your belly, and your face went for a ride through the dirt. I was there a few times since I got saved from the wild life. I see God is working with you. What! He is not doing anything with me! He's ignoring me. He is choosing to work with another fellow horse, and I never got a chance to get started. I don't understand how He could do this to me? I don't need this kind of treatment! I'm going back for a day in the wild life! The visiting fellow horse said, are you sure that's what you want to do? Yes, said the baby. I am no longer excited about what is happening here. Besides, our Great Breaker and

Trainer hurt my feelings when He suddenly pulled me down on my belly, and my face went full speed through the dirt. Let me out of the center of this corral. Where's the gate? At this time, the visiting fellow horse is on his knees with his nose tipped downward into the front of his neck.

(The preacher enters in) Time for intercessory prayer (Meanwhile, back at the corral), the visiting fellow horse speaks without lifting his nose from the front of his neck. Which gate do you want? There are two gates. There's the wide one, and there's the narrow one. Oh, I guess you want the wide one because the narrow one is for coming in only! If you start roaming from the center of the corral, you will find the wide gate real easy. So, the big baby Christian horse starts to gait toward the wide gate. He gaits, and he gaits until he reaches the wide gate. He has left the center of our Great Breaker and Trainers corral. As he gets to the wide gate, he notices that it opens before he can push it. It swings open automatically. Maybe our Great Breaker and Trainer has His own Genie? So, the big baby Christian horse starts gaiting through the wide gate. As he leaves, he turns and sees the gate swing closed. He notices that God has a couple of hired hands sitting on top of the gate. They are calm and relaxed and have a radiant shine on their faces. (The preacher enters in) the Lord guards the kingdom children with many of His obedient Angels. (Psalm 103:20)

(Meanwhile, back to the excursion from the corral.) As the big baby wanders back into the wild life, he senses something is very different. He feels like he does not fit in as he did before. He comes to a big tree, and standing next to it is what seems to be a very attractive filly, a beautiful young female horse! She has her eyelids blinking up and down and her lips open. She is moving her neck with a wiggle and turning around in a circular manner displaying her fine figure. She is luring him over to the tree. (The preacher enters in) Does that sound familiar to anyone? She lures him over to the tree! Here we have a temptation going on, which is by a tree. Trouble is coming!

(Meanwhile, back to the filly and the big baby Christian horse.) The baby starts to sweat and thinks about what could happen if he makes a neck connection with the filly. He moves closer to make the neck connection with her. Suddenly, she vanishes, and he hears a roar! Up in the tree, a huge mountain lion is screaming for horse meat. Then he realizes the attractive filly was really a night-mare! The night-mare was working for the mountain lion! The big baby senses a fear he never had before. The mountain lion jumps from the tree and lands on the middle of his back with his claws around his neck. The big baby starts running for his life, saying get off my back; I belong to our Great Breaker and Trainer. He will get you off my back. He runs with record speed back toward the corral.

(The preacher enters in) I Peter 5:8, NIV. Be self-controlled and alert your enemy, the devil, prowls around like a roaring lion looking for someone to devour. (Meanwhile, racing back to the corral) the big baby reaches the narrow gate at the corral and leaps over it before it opens by the hired hands. The mountain lion is still on His back with his claws around the baby's neck. He runs to the center of the corral, and the mountain lion lets go and departs with record speed out of the corral.

(The preacher enters in) James 4:7 NASB, submit therefore to God resist the devil and he will flee from you. This is the same baby Christian horse who was condemning the excellent performing horse because he ran from the mountain lion in the wild life. He said he was not afraid of the mountain lions and that he never ran from them. This is a lesson of judging others wrongly and a bitter root judgment from God. It is also the consequence of the poison of pride that brought death to the whole world and all living creatures.

(Meanwhile, back at the corral) The big baby Christian horse is now in the center of the corral. The visiting fellow horse who was with him when he decided to take the excursion into the wild life was still on his knees with his nose tipped downward into the front of his neck.

(The preacher enters in) 1st Thessalonians 5:17- Pray without ceasing. This interpretation from the visiting fellow horse was as literal as it could get! (Meanwhile, back at the corral) The visiting fellow horse looked up and saw that the big baby had returned to the corral. They rubbed necks together in fellowship, rejoicing at God's deliverance from the devil. Another faithful rescue has taken place! The visiting fellow horse spoke to the new baby; are you ready to learn from your recent excursion into the wild life? Yes! Yes! Please tell me everything, so it does not happen again. I want to say I learned my lesson from our Great Breaker and Trainer!

The visiting fellow horse began to speak. When God was going to start training you, you said you were going to do great things. You said you would show Him and the excellent performing horse what great really was. You were comparing yourself to the excellent performing horse and putting him down verbally. You boasted about your ability. This was a big mistake. You are not great, and you must never speak against a fellow horse in a demeaning way. The excellent performing horse is not great either. I am not great. My gift of counsel comes directly from our Great Breaker and Trainer. None of the fellow horses in this whole corral are great. None of us can show what great is in our abilities. Only our Great Breaker and Trainer is GREAT! Him and Him alone! He gives us the ability and skill and wants to live His life through us. We become prize show horses for His Glory. A moment of silence sets in; I have a question, says the baby Christian horse.

How did the excellent performing horse get where he did? Tell me about his amazing change. The visiting fellow horse starts to answer his question. He started by using those two big ears of his. And when our Great Breaker and Trainer first tightened the rope around his neck he… Wait a minute... Why don't you ask him, yourself?

He is running the race set before him, but he is not in competition with you. His only competition is somewhere under those four big shoes he is wearing. He would be happy to tell you where he got where he did. So the new baby Christian horse went over to talk to the excellent performing fellow horse he knew in the wild life. Hello, pal, remember me? Sure I do, said the excellent performer. I rejoiced when I saw you get pulled into the corral. I was on my way over to greet you and rub necks with you yesterday. But you left the middle of the corral and started walking away. When I saw you going toward the edge of the corral, I knew I could not follow you because I don't want to leave the center of the corral. Where were you going, or maybe I should not even ask? Please, don't ask said the baby. That is all behind me now! I came over to ask you how you got where you did with our Great Breaker and Trainer. I would consider it a privilege to tell you said an excellent performer. All new Christians need the proper guidance. I will start with several points of truth we all must practice in our new and abundant life.

1. When our Great Breaker and Trainer first tightened the rope around my neck I knew something wonderful was going to happen. I said to myself; He can't possibly hurt me with this rope. He used it to rescue me from the wild life where I would have surely died. You see, without the rope around my neck to keep me under His control I know how wild I can become.
2. I thank Him every day for my new life no matter what is happening.
3. I say, my God do what you want with me I belong to you. You gave me the abundant life and you paid the price to rescue me.
4. I say, Great Breaker and Trainer I trust you to do great things with my life. It will be a privilege and a pleasure to watch YOU work!
5. I often say, okay Master, You know what is best for me.
6. I walk quietly and wait for His instructions learning His word and praying.
7. I show Him I am satisfied with whatever ability He chooses to display through me. It's His choice and apart from Him I can do nothing that is really fruitful.

8. I rejoice when I see another fellow horse performing in an excellent way. I know he is reflecting God's glory and ability.

9. I tell Him I love Him and I want to grow in submission to His authority.

10. I constantly ask Him to fill me with His love and empowerment so others can see He is over me, through me, and in me.

It is my yielded witness to make Him known to the wild ones without salvation and better known to some of my fellow horses in this corral. You have now heard how I got where I did with our Great Breaker and Trainer. It is His Great Love for us and His Mercy and Grace that gives us this wonderful privilege! The Big Baby Christian Horse has learned very much and he is ready to move toward maturity by putting the days of his youth behind him. He is ready to move on to a disciplined life under God's guidance, wisdom, love and authority. (The preacher enters in) I will leave you all with these words from our Great Breaker and Trainer.

1. Pride goes before destruction and a haughty spirit before a fall. Prov.16:18 NIV)

2. God opposes the proud but gives grace to the humble-- James 4:6 NIV

3. We must decrease so He can increase. Ref. John 3:30

4. A man's pride will bring him low, but a humble spirit will obtain honor. Proverbs 29:23 NASB

5. Jesus said, if anyone would come after Me, he must deny himself and take up his cross and follow Me. Luke 9:23 NASB

(Meanwhile, back at the corral) Time passed, and the new Christian horse was no longer a baby in the corral. He was convinced he needed to cooperate with our Great Breaker and Trainer. He started to reflect excellence in his new life. God had control of him, and he was walking in victory. He learned the Christian life is always being humble, submissive, and obedient! He was very grateful to our Great Breaker and Trainer. He was very grateful to his fellow horses, who helped him learn the way life really works.

(Preacher's final exhortation) This is why we must assemble as God's people. We must teach each other and love each other. We own a relationship with each other, a strong spiritual bond as the body of Jesus Christ. We individually submit to one another and share in God's life. Our objective is not our personal success. Our objective is to be the servants we became when we were saved. (Romans 6:18) Our faith in Him is our victory in life.

(Meanwhile, back at the corral for the last time) In this final scene at the corral, the new victorious and successful Christian horse is talking with his good friend and new brother, the excellent performing horse. He tells him he wants our Great Breaker and Trainer, our God, to keep the rope around him permanently! His excellent friend and new brother says that is a great attitude to have. But there will come a time when the rope will no longer be necessary. There will come a time for a new corral without a fence when God completes His glorious work building His final family of believers for all eternity. If you think this corral is great, wait until you see the next one!

Key Note: Don't be like a stubborn horse but receive the discipline and love God has for all of us! See Hebrews 12: 5-14 in all Bible versions! Final Note: We take God's love into the wild life to do our part to rescue others into His coral. As for them, they may listen and turn to God. As for us, we never join them and turn back to the old wild life!

The Trees of the Field will Clap their Hands

There is so much to learn from the observation of trees. This is an exclusive spiritual study of trees and all they can tell us about our wonderful Creator.

1. Ref. Genesis 2:9, the start of trees in creation. Isiah 55:12b says all the trees of field will clap their hands. Let's see what this means. I asked God to show me more about trees for I was always looking at them after my salvation. Ref. John 15:1-8 in this passage Jesus tells us He is our Vine and we are His branches. Much of what we learn comes from observations in the reality we see and experience. Here is a brief outline of this writing. Jesus is the Vine!)

A. A good tree compared to a bad tree

B. A bad branch and a branch by itself

C. Survey Time from Christ the Vine!

A. 1. When a tree is good they all have the right life source to grow.

A. 2. The branches of a good tree grow close together. They touch each other and they mingle together. They give support to each other. They share the rain and the sun and produce fruit in a cluster. Rejoicing in the light and shining as a whole tree no branches stand out above any others. Only the Vine stands out as the power source that gives all strength and beauty to the tree. The branches bend without breaking when the storm comes and they are stopped from falling by leaning on the other branches that are close to them.

A. 3. No one says look at that beautiful branch. They say look at that beautiful tree. There is unity and order, togetherness, peace and beauty. The branches are abiding in the Vine that gives them life. They rely on the Vine to keep them from being uprooted or detached from their peaceful position on the tree.

A. 4. The good tree grows at a slow rate and if the branches could speak they would tell you they are never in a hurry! Looking at a good tree gives us the message of patience.

A. 5. The storms of life will test the branches and toss them back and forth but as long as they have enough of the life flow from the Vine they make it through the storm.

A. 6. Sometimes the branches get disturbed from things other than the storm. A prowling cat or a speedy squirrel might jump on top of them. Are there any squirrels in your life? They are hungry creatures looking for food or, as the term has been applied to some people, someone who needs to find a real purpose and meaning by discovering their real life flow. They need to place their trust in the real life flow of the Vine before they can become someone who is trustworthy.

A. 7. Maybe a jumbo raven has landed on one of the branches and caused a big disturbance and a big mess. Every branch will get dumped on periodically. But, the Vine has determined that the raven may still land on the branch. The branch must be patient and wait for the raven to complete his visit. The branch can't throw the raven off or complain about its company. Complaining would not change anything. The branch often has little to say about the good and bad things that happen to it. The branch can only abide in the Vine. All the disturbances will pass and the Vine will give strength and endurance to the branches. A mature branch may invite the squirrel to a visit and the squirrel could even stretch out and take a nap. A mature branch will have fruit to share with the squirrel and make the situation very peaceful and loving. The squirrel may tell his friends he met a very friendly branch and invite them along the next time he visits. Matthew 13:32 NIV tells us how a very small mustard seed will grow a big and fruitful tree and welcome the birds of the air to perch on its branches. So we, who are the branches of the true Vine, can welcome all the squirrelly ones! All of us can be a little squirrelly with the fallen nature we have. A haven of rest is only from God. And the true Vine produces branches that extend His rest and love to all. In Matthew 5:44 NIV. Jesus says love your enemies and pray for those who persecute you. Jesus takes it to the highest level of His love. Jesus made himself available and vulnerable to do God's will. This included being rejected and abused by those who would not receive Him. The branches do the same. Jesus embraced the Fathers will to carry out salvation for the world. Sacrificial and unconditional love was offered to all people.

A. 8. The branches give an excellent example of servitude. You submit to the Vine and whatever He allows we give thanks in all things. The inconvenience or trial will test and develop our character. Perseverance in character makes us complete. Ref. (James 1: 2-4.) Evil can only be conquered by God's love. Give thanks and praise in all things. Accepting who you are in Christ means serving others as He has served us. Each branch has been given a different position on the Vine. Your placement has been determined by the Vine and you have no say as to where you want to be on the tree. This relates to our gifting from the Holy Spirit. As He determines He gives spiritual gifts to us. A branch can't say I want to be in a different place on the tree. Abiding in the Vine is a privilege and we have the ability God gives and provides as a whole body. The body of the tree is all the branches in every direction and position. The one thing they all have in common is they all grow upward and go outward.

A. 9. Each branch becomes a living part of the Vine and is more than a servant. We become sons and daughters of God and we are eternally adopted to our new Father. The Vine owns its branches. Thank God we are part of the tree of life!

A. 10. A branch does not always know what will happen next but there is one thing that always takes place. They have an assignment to grow and make the Vine known as the only life source. We tell other dead branches that they can become part of the Vine of Life! The bigger branches bring other branches to the Vine and they give witness to baby branches by the process of multiplication.

A. 11. The branches drop seeds on the ground and the wind can blow them to other places. This can cause God to water them and more trees can grow with the same Vine until there is a whole field of trees. The trees of the field of the Kingdom of God are all the church congregations that meet in each different place. Christ is the eternal Vine and power source of every branch and every tree of God's field.

A. 12. Proverbs 11:30, NASB, says the fruit of the righteous is a tree of life and he who is wise wins souls. (Adding more branches to the tree)

A. 13. The Vine works through all the branches on a good tree and the branches are very close to each other. They are flexible. They bend to help and give support to other branches. Here is an illustration I came up with; A box of spaghetti; each piece is very hard and not flexible before it is cooked. One piece could be snapped in half very easily. Take a few more right next to each other and it gains strength. It is a little harder to break. Take a whole handful and it is very hard to break them in half. And these have no flexibility to begin with. The branches on a good tree are filled with the flow of the Vine and even one can be hard to break. It will bend being filled with the Vine but one can be broken. Imagine a whole handful of branches filled with the Vine and try to break them. They will not be broken. If you are a branch and Jesus is your Vine and you stay close to the other branches in Jesus we will not be broken. We have supernatural strength by abiding in the Vine of life Jesus the Lord! We are powerful as a church when we stay together and abide in Him.

A. 14. Tarzan was known for swinging on the vines of the trees to travel through the jungle. They were filled with a powerful life flow like heavy ropes to swing on. He did not fall and die by one of the vines breaking. His last words were who greased the viiiiiiiinnnnnnneeeeee?

A. 15. All branches filled with the Vine will always bounce back when they are interfered with. They are resilient and they maintain their position by abiding in the Vine. Ever hear the expression don't get all bent out of shape? It means don't be bothered or disturbed to the point where you can't take it and let it defeat you. Be resilient and ready to bounce back every time you feel like you're getting knocked down. My brother had a rubber plastic blow up doll when we were very young. It stood up filled with air and it had some heavy substance in the bottom of it to keep it balanced in a standing position. If you punched it real hard it would fall all the way down backward and come flying back up and balance itself. It had a face of a boy on it with a very big smile. I think they called it a Joe Paluka doll. We knocked it down and punched it over and over while we were laughing, and it kept coming up and giving us a big smile. It was saying you can't hurt me! I am resilient because I have a strong foundation to keep me standing up! If I fall I will keep getting back up and you won't knock me out! Sounds like the foundation we have in our Vine of life. For though a righteous man falls seven times he rises again. (Proverbs 24:16a NIV.) Smile if Jesus is your Vine and your foundation! You have what it takes to get back up after a brief fall. Keep a smile on your face you are secure in Jesus. Refer to Matthew 10:28, it tells us no one can stop or kill our soul. That is the Vine of life in us! Have patience and endurance God will finish what he started.

A. 16. The branches of a good tree do not compare themselves in a negative way to each other. They work together to complete the tree. Accepting one another in Christ and being close and friendly should stop all immature comparisons. A branch can complement another branch by saying, I like the new leaves you're wearing they look real good on you. Or the fruit cluster you have looks very tasty.

You could say I like the way you're growing, and they may say, well, nothing beats a bud! We live in kindness to all our brothers and sisters speaking words of love.

A. 17. With a good tree you can't see through the branches. There is no distance between the branches. There should be no distance between brothers and sisters in the Lord either. We are to love one another as we are commanded.

When a tree is bad there is distance between the branches, and they all seem to be going their own way. A bad tree is when the branches have rejected the Vine and Christ is not allowed to be the life flow the way He wants to be. On a bad tree it seems like the branches are wanting to stand out by themselves. They want distance between themselves and the other branches. This takes us to Matthew 15:13. Jesus says all plants that His Father did not plant will be uprooted. God sustains all life but without Jesus the life is temporary. The tree will look out of balance and without unity. There is no hope for unity or abundant life without Jesus as the Vine.

A 18. Remember there is a unique difference between each branch on a good tree even though they are very close and unified with each other. The Vine has positioned them in one place and given them a unique gift to produce more branches. One will spread growth differently than another. One will serve more visitors and one will reach out to keep producing more buds by sowing seeds to promote the Vine. The Vine uses different functions for the branches as the Vine determines. A tree is only as strong as its roots. When Christ is the root of the Vine the tree is grounded deeper than we can imagine. The root is eternally alive and can never die. His roots have no end and His roots have always existed. The eternal God created all things and only God can make a tree!

Part B---- (A bad branch and a branch by itself)

In a fallen world we see malfunctions of what God intended because of the curse in nature and on all men and women born from the first Adam.

Suppose you see a tree with a big branch sticking out going directly sideways while other branches are showing more unity. This branch is growing away from the others. It is a malfunction of growth, and it is way longer than the other branches. How would people respond or what would some of them say?

1. It is really strange the way this branch is growing.
2. It has no other branches near it and no new branches showing.

3. It is not producing anything fruitful. It is rebelling against the natural order.
4. It is seeking its own direction. It is like the tree is rejecting it.
5. It will not share the light and the rain with the other branches.
6. It has no company to lean on or to support it; no contact with the other branches.

What are people's reactions to it?

1. It does not fit the tree it does not belong there.
2. Going a step farther it should be cut off.
3. This looks like some good firewood.
4. Someone could put a swing on it and it will not disturb the rest of the tree.
5. But what if a chubby, fat mash potato lover swings on it. Is it strong enough?
6. This branch should have cooperated with the Vine and the good branches.
7. It is counter to natural order and destined to be ruined or cut off.

We conclude it is isolated from the other branches and out of contact with what's normal. It's not conforming to the Vines plan. Since it is being referred to as a person in this writing, it could indicate- being slothful, showing apathy and ignorance, in fear or unbelief, and drying out and dying. The Bible says a branch that does not bear fruit will be taken away in the kingdom of God. (John 15:2)

Another way a branch can go bad is when a disease comes upon it. In a fallen world, a pestilence of darkness could attack a branch on a tree. Insects, bees, wasps, or leeches may be sucking the life flow out of the branch. Being separated from the Vine makes a branch vulnerable to attack in this fallen world. There are also times when you see short and tiny branches dangling that are attached to the tree directly or attached to some of the bigger branches, and it appears that they never grew correctly or cooperated with the Vine. These little danglers get pruned off the tree. Maybe the little dangler said I do not want to grow up. I don't like such a slow process, so I will not get with the program. Their growth has been completely stunted. A branch is also bad when it tries to control how another branch should be growing. Referring to people here, the branch is exceeding its limitations and trying to do only what the Vine can do. You can make suggestions, but you can't force another branch to grow, thinking you can do it in your own strength. We can't take the place of the Vine in how it grows in other branches. We can only abide in the Vine and ask the Vine to help other branches. Is anyone trying to be God in some other person's life?

Part C: Survey Time from Christ the Vine!

20 Questions

What kind of branch are you? If you're brave you can keep score.

1. Are you a branch that abides in the Vine morning, noon, and night? Are you confiding and abiding or causing some dividing?
2. Are you permitting the Vine to make you strong? Is your situation defined as Alive and then Thrive or very Bleak and very Weak?
3. Do you unite with the other branches and are you reflecting the light as part of a whole tree? Or, are you one of those shady characters?
4. Do you stay close to the other branches in times of adversity? When the storm comes do you wish you could escape or do you hold on to the other branches and cling to the Vine?
5. If you see some other branches, sometimes, look like a weeping willow do you weep with them and show empathy and compassion?
6. Do you always go the direction that the Vine has planned for you or do you try to go your own direction and disregard the plan of the Vine? Do you go with the righteous flow or do you often refuse and discover you will lose?
7. Are you growing up and going out to produce baby branches? Are you adding branches to the family or only thinking about your own desires. Have you accepted your responsibility or neglected it to the point of futility?
8. Do you nurture and strengthen other branches or are you too busy to take the time for it? Are you a spiritual prig or a stuck up twig? Or, are you a fruit bearing fig helping others get big?
9. Do you guide and train baby branches to abide in the Vine so they can grow up and know they are fine? Or, do you put them down complaining time after time?
10. If a baby branch starts to fall do you reach out to catch it trying to stop the fall? Or, are you too proud to come down to the ones who are small?

11. Do you feed the baby branches enough of the Vine flowing through you so they can grow up and go out to produce their own baby branches? Or, are you starting to chill and forgetting Gods will? John 6:40.
12. Do you have enough of the Vine to do Godly things, showing His love and the new life He brings? Or, are you in the world focused on temporary things ignoring the danger and the death of its sting?
13. Are you a branch that knows exactly where you fit on the Vine? Or, are you envious of another branch and its position? Are you satisfied with where you're at? Or, are you an envious, spoiled, conceited brat? Please forgive me for that I don't mean to attack; but know that we all are experiencing lack!
14. Are you a branch that tries to hoard all the light and rain water or do you share it with the other branches? Are you generous and kind or has the darkness made you blind? Are you a real life giver or a faker and a taker?
15. Are you a branch that has allowed the enemy to build a stronghold and hang his nest right on top of you? Are you being stung by the enemy permitting him to tap all your strength and resources? Are you resisting with a fight or doing nothing to make things right?
16. Are you a branch that has allowed a disease to come upon you because of deliberate and wrongful action? Is there a disease eating the life flow out of you? Do you turn to God to repent or is entertaining evil your intent?
17. For the whole congregation, are you a tree that could break or burn easily or a tree that is filled with the Vine? Are you complacent, lifeless and brittle or helping dead branches find their acquittal?
18. Is this congregation a tree that is growing to full maturity or is it always like wintertime? Are you stagnate and cold giving Satan a foothold? Or, are you producing much fruit being wise and astute?
19. Is this congregation a tree of the field that can clap its hands? Are you rejoicing in the Vine and all His commands? Are you abiding and obeying finding joy that will last, not letting go of the Vine with a very tight grasp?

20. Is the Vine your only true story? Does the Vine get all the glory? Will you sing and clap forever for the privilege of His treasure? We have Eternal life without measure with our God for His good pleasure!

It's not me it's Mr. Dunamis!

This writing is going to be an interview a reporter is giving to an undercover agent, who I am giving the name of Mr. Dunamis. There is no real Mr. Dunamis. I did not want to tell the reporter the agent's real name until the reporter is ready to receive him openly. The undercover agent will be discovered during the interview. The undercover agent is doing evangelism during the interview, and He wants to save the reporter and make him a citizen of heaven. The undercover agent is a person real Christians know well. He is a person who never talks about himself, but He speaks clearly about two other persons and tells many people about the two persons He knows best. The undercover agent is The Holy Spirit, the third person of the Trinity who is equally God Himself! The reporter has a background of association to the Christian faith but never discovered the complete truth about God's salvation. At least it has been that way until now! The reporter will start his interview and is in for a real surprise! I will refer to him as the Interviewer in this writing and to the Holy Spirit as Mr. Dunamis. I felt extremely led by God to write this! This inspirational writing touches our heart's knowledge about the function of the Holy Spirit! Creative to the imagination and showing God's attributes; I hope you get edified in your soul from it. I hope you can catch the humor of God. (Now we will hear from the Interviewer!)

I want to give you some background on Mr. Dunamis. I was assigned to interview him. He is a humble fellow who, when I asked for an interview, said, I never speak about myself, but in this case, I will make an exception.

Interviewer: Mr. Dunamis, when and where were you born?

Mr. Dunamis: I wasn't born; I have always existed.

Interviewer: How do you measure how old you are?

Mr. Dunamis: I am before all time and after all time, without measure.

Interviewer: You mean you never celebrate a birthday?

Mr. Dunamis: No, so I never complained about not getting a present!

Interviewer: If you never complained you must be a real gentleman!

Mr. Dunamis: I am the kindest of gentlemen.

Interviewer: Where do you live?

Mr. Dunamis: I live wherever I am welcomed or invited. On the other hand I go wherever I please whenever I please.

Interviewer: That doesn't sound much like a gentleman to me. (Mr. Dunamis said, back off pal! And for some reason I obeyed.)

Interviewer: What do you do for a living?

Mr. Dunamis: I work so that everyone else can live.

Interviewer: Man, you must have supernatural strength. If you work so that everyone else can live, that includes a vast amount of people.

Do you have any idea how many people are in the world?

Mr. Dunamis: Yes! And I work for every one of them.

Interviewer: Don't you ever get tired?

Mr. Dunamis: Never! But if I could get tired it might come from answering all your questions.

Interviewer: Please forgive me, but I sense something very different about you as a person. I believe many people who don't know you may want to know you. They may need someone like you in their life.

Mr. Dunamis: Forgiveness from me is free and you don't have to say please. Just be sincere. Oh, by the way, I will never get tired of all your questions. Ask and you will receive. I was simply testing your heart to see if you really wanted to know me and if you had a genuine interest in having other people know me.

Interviewer: Do you ever get angry?

Mr. Dunamis: Yes, usually when I am at places I am not welcomed or invited. When I'm at these places I must control my temper because I love everyone much more than they love me.

Interviewer: Wow! You're the kindest gentleman of all and you show love more than anyone else? You're a very complete person!

Mr. Dunamis: Yes and Amen!

Interviewer: Mr. Dunamis do you consider yourself to be intelligent and wise?

Mr. Dunamis: I never boast but my honest and true answer is Yes, I am. I gave King Solomon all the wisdom he possessed and I gave Einstein all the knowledge he possessed and it didn't even dent my reservoir.

Interviewer: You are telling me you're that intelligent and wise?

Mr. Dunamis: Without boasting and being very honest I know everything. I'm Omniscient. I can also be everywhere at the same time since people measure time. I'm omnipresent. And I am the ultimate power of the universe. I'm omnipotent.

Interviewer: Mr. Dunamis I'm not sure you are giving it to me straight. (He instantly responded, back off pal! (And for some reason I obeyed) I said, Let me get this straight. You're the kindest, strongest, most loving gentleman of all. You are almighty, all knowing and everywhere at the same time?

Mr. Dunamis: Yes and double Amen!

Interviewer: If these things are true, and I am starting to believe you're not lying to me, then everyone should obey you at all times, doing always only what you want them to do. Is that correct? SILENCE, There is no immediate response.

Interviewer: Mr. Dunamis are you still with me? No answer and Mr. Dunamis begins to weep. Then He speaks again, "there are many that do not obey me. They don't do what I would like them to do."

Interviewer: Well, make them obey you. Make them do whatever you want them to do. Rub them out or snuff them out in a split second if they refuse to listen to you.

Mr. Dunamis: No! No! That would not be love. Each person must choose to love or hate me, to obey or disobey me. It wouldn't be love if they are forced against their will to do what I desire from them. The Father and the Son and I agree that this is the way it should be.

Interviewer: Wait a minute Mr. Dunamis. This talk of the Father and the Son is getting a bit confusing. Are you talking about God the Father and Jesus Christ the Son?

Mr. Dunamis: Yes I am.

Interviewer: You have the nerve to include yourself with the Christian God? Are you equal with God?

Mr. Dunamis: I AM!

Interviewer: Are you giving it to me straight? Mr. Dunamis said, Back of pal! (And for some reason that was becoming increasingly clear- I obeyed!)

Interviewer: When I was growing up and went to church, on occasion, I heard them talk about God the Father and Jesus Christ the Son but never about any Mr. Dunamis.

Mr. Dunamis: When you were growing up did you hear or believe you could know Jesus Christ as your personal Lord and Savior?

Interviewer: Only the disciples and a few women named Mary knew Jesus personally. (Mr. Dunamis puts his hands over his eyes and shakes his head back and forth)

Mr. Dunamis: Have you ever heard of the Holy Spirit?

Interviewer: Well, they mentioned that name a few times at the end of prayers. Otherwise, no, I didn't hear too much about him.

Mr. Dunamis: I did not reveal my real name to you at the beginning of this interview. I am the Holy Spirit, the third person of the Trinity. Do you know that I can teach you the truth about Jesus Christ the Son of God? Do you know that Jesus Christ is the exact image of the Invisible God? We three are ONE; God the Father, God the Son, God the Holy Spirit.

Interviewer: (All of a sudden I became very nervous. I was under conviction because I was hearing from God Himself)

Interviewer: Now just wait one more minute here, who's doing this interview? You or me? You seem to be taking over! How did you get control? Who gave you the control? (Mr. Dunamis said, back off pal! And wouldn't you know it, I was compelled to obey—again!)

Mr. Dunamis: Sit Down Mr. Interviewer

Interviewer: Yes Sir! (My eyes were wide open)

Mr. Dunamis: Listen to Me carefully.

Interviewer: I'm all ears, ah, Mr. Holy Spirit, ah I mean Mr. Dunamis. Ah I mean Holy Spirit, Sir.

Mr. Dunamis: Dunamis is a Greek word which means ability, power, abundance, strength, mighty miracle working energy. I am the Holy Spirit who possesses ultimate power. I am the master and maker of miracles. I am the power and reality of God working in human lives. Do you, Mr. Interviewer, know that you must be born again by the power of Holy Spirit to receive eternal life in the Kingdom of Heaven?

Interviewer: What is this to be born of the Spirit? I've already been born once from my mother. How can I be born again?

Mr. Dunamis: (He raises his voice) Ah, Ha, now I can go on to talk about the ONE, I usually talk about. You have been born once of the flesh. You must be born of the Spirit. You have been born in sin against God because the sin nature is of the flesh. You must be born again! You are dead because of sin and because God is Spirit only those who have been born of the Spirit can know and eventually see God. The reason for death is sin. Sin is disobedience to God and His Word. The Father sent His Son, Jesus Christ, to take away the sin of the world and destroy the works of the devil. The devil was the first sinner. In his pride he acted arrogantly against us, The Holy Trinity. It is hard to fathom how he could have been so stupid and foolish. All of mankind fell when Adam and Eve gave in to, Satan, the devil's temptation in the Garden of Eden. They disobeyed God's command. Pride leads to disobedience, which is sin and this is what kills humanity. Jesus came as the perfect, sinless, holy sacrifice for all of human sin. Interviewer: This is all getting very interesting. I'm glad you are taking charge of this interview.

Mr. Dunamis: Yes! And triple Amen, and hallelujah!

Interviewer: Exactly, how do you make a dead spirit alive to the knowledge of the reality of God?

Mr. Dunamis: You must receive Jesus Christ into your life as personal Lord and Savior through faith. In your heart you must be truly sorry for all the sins you have committed against God. You must acknowledge Christ as the Son of God who died as the substitute for your sins and redeemed you with His shed blood on the cross. You must welcome Him into your heart and life. Sin will be removed as you realize it as sin and disobedience to God's Word. Make your confession of Jesus Christ as your personal Lord and Savior now! God will then send Me, Mr. Dunamis, The

Holy Spirit, the Spirit of Father and the Son, Jesus Christ, the Spirit of truth and power, the heavenly helper into your life to dwell in you. I regenerate the hearts of men and women and give them a personal relationship with the Father and the Son Jesus who is the mediator between God and every human person. I will transform men and women into the image of the Father and the Son for we are ONE! Right now you can have a life changing experience by receiving power and victory over sin in your life. Furthermore, you will have peace that passes all understanding. You will be enabled to love everyone. Even the most unlovely people can be loved by My Spirit through you. Wisdom and knowledge will descend from above and you will have joy unspeakable and full of glory! I can make you a citizen of heaven. You will worship in spirit and in truth. Accept Christ and you will forever be grateful for His salvation and want to talk with others about Him. You will learn about Jesus and how to live like Him. Holiness, with humility and righteousness will give you confidence that you never had before, and you will want to tell others of your soul's salvation and that you are a recreated child of God!

Interviewer: Mr. Dunamis, ah, I mean Holy Spirit stop! I want to make a decision or Jesus Christ right now!

Mr. Dunamis: My interview has not been in vain! Glory to God!

Interviewer: I prayed the prayer of faith and received Christ into my life right then and there. What a wonderful miracle it was. After a short time people started to ask me all sorts of questions: Why are you so happy? How can you love people the way you do? How are you accomplishing the things you are doing now? Why don't you get angry like you were before? When did you stop the profanity we use to hear from you? Why aren't you prideful like you were before? Where did you get such wisdom? How did you get so strong? What do you do that allows you to act and show love, joy, peace, patience, kindness, goodness, faithfulness, gentleness, and self-control? How do you do it? When they ask me, I just smile and say, "It's not me it's Mr. Dunamis!" The power of God in me! The miracle worker! The Holy Spirit has come to indwell my heart! He tells me about Jesus and enables me to live like Him. Christ lives His life through me today! It's very real and equally wonderful. Jesus said, He is the way the truth and the life and that no one comes to God the Father apart from Him. (Ref. John 14:6) For everyone who needs to know Jesus Christ personally, Mr. Dunamis is available for an interview. He will connect you to God the Father in heaven through His Son Jesus Christ.

Mr. Dunamis: Yes and quadruple Amen! Glory and hallelujah! I.B.M.D.

After hearing about Mr. Dunamis you can know what the I.B.M.D means at the end of the writing. It means (Inspired by Mr. Dunamis.) It shows no irreverence to God at all and it brings me to a deeper level of intimacy with the love of my life. I was given the writing at 1:30 in the morning while I was suffering from a severe ear infection. I sat at my kitchen table and felt His presence very strongly from within me. I started pushing the pen and had no thoughts or plan to write it. It was making me laugh and cry because I was being used by the Lord. I could feel no pain from my ear infection while the Holy Spirit was involved in a very tangible way. I was enjoying His power, love and sense of humor. He is without my doubt the most complete person and everything the Bible says about God and more. He was conveying the Father and the Son and their love, power and humor to me. He was showing me that we have a God who can humble himself and laugh with us resulting in an overwhelming privilege to us. The three persons of the Trinity are very real and their love is deeper than we can fathom. I like to call God the Cosmic Trio that rules the universe! The God of One essence in the other centered love of three persons in all of its perfection and power. His active presence can cause us to put everything else aside as He chooses to visit us with an intervention of inspiration from the highest Dimension of Love and life possible. Nothing else matters when you know God, Himself, is allowing you to hear Him so clearly by His Spirit speaking directly to your heart and mind. It is the greatest privilege a man or woman can receive. I thank Him from my whole heart! Brother in Christ, Jim Elarde.

The Preliminary Hearing of Faith Members of the Highest Court!

Hosea 4:1 (NLT) The Lord has filed a lawsuit against you, saying: There is no faithfulness, no kindness, and no knowledge of God in your land. This is saying there will be a courtroom hearing. The case against every person will be judged by the truth in the only Supreme Court that exists forever. The Highest Court: at the Throne of God. God, in His loving kindness and patience, is giving people a chance to have the guilty verdict taken away! The Gospel, the good news of Jesus Christ, is a preliminary hearing that precedes the final hearing, where there will be no chance for acquittal. Presenting the Gospel message of Jesus Christ is done by people who have become members of the highest court. As children of God, we have been seated in heaven with Christ and commanded to bring reconciliation crucial to all people. We will first examine how God takes on many roles as He chooses to work to save all people.

1. The Holy Spirit starts out like a private investigator, a great detective who examines all the motives and thoughts of every person's heart. He sees all the inherent evil and every wrong act. Proverbs 15:3 NASB Version says the eyes of the Lord are in every place, watching the evil and the good. He has been called the hound of heaven by some people of the Christian Faith. He tries to convict people to turn to God and admit they need desperate help. He will work in the conscience to point out things that are not right and work to show us there is a perfect moral God who has made us. My father watched the T.V. series Columbo, which was very popular. Columbo used to get under a person's skin in a way that would unravel them in his effort to solve the crime. He would leave the person he was questioning and then keep coming back and saying oh, just one more thing. The Holy Spirit wants to get under people's skin and to the real issues of the heart that God knows are not right. When you peel an egg, there is a thin skin you have to get under for the egg to come out right. When you don't get under that skin correctly, the egg crumbles and breaks. God makes an effort to get under our skin so we can come out right before Him by admitting we need Him. The conscience of a man is where the lamp of the Lord is searching to reveal Himself. He calls people in their conscience. (Proverbs 20:27)

2. God is also like the chief of police who knows there is enough evidence to book people for their sins. The only difference is God does not want to lock them up! God wants to set them free! The Word of God sets people free. God says to all his Gospel messengers; Book them for their sins but don't lock them up! Set them free! If you are a believer, open your Bible and hold it against your heart. Say, I've been booked. I am free! God wants to book all people with the Word of God.

3. God is also like the Head of the F.B.I. He has wanted posters all over the world. As a result of His ownership, we should all turn ourselves in.

God's F.B.I means>> FOR BEST INHERITANCE!

Wanted

Transgressor of God's Law! Dead to Sin! Alive to God! This is a recent photo of the transgressor. If you have any information leading to the capture of this person, notify the Highest Authority! This person was last seen just a few moments ago!

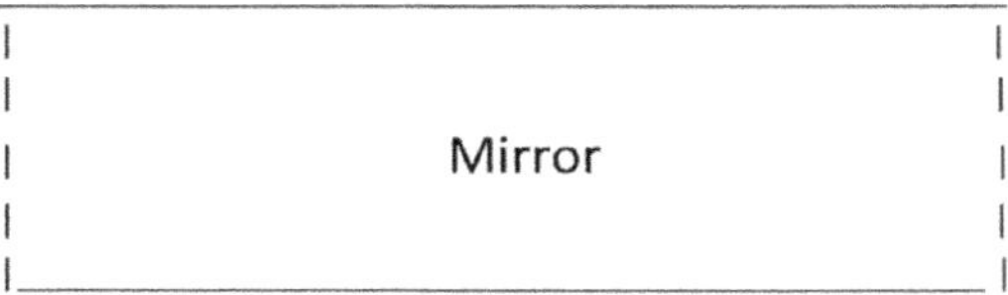

Eternal Reward!

Whoever turns this person in by the free will choice of faith in Jesus Christ will receive an eternal reward that will exceed all the riches the world has to offer! Jesus has paid the price for this transgressor by dying in his or her place. The capture of this person to God who owns them through creation and wants to own them through redemption will result in their release by the Highest Court! They will be pardoned and set free with just one sentence outstanding. They will become servants of God through Jesus Christ. He will be Lord and Savior of their life. By this eternal life they will become an adopted child of the One and only God! Take heed to this offer! If you return to Him you will collect your own wonderful bounty! The highest price has been paid for your eternal life! Is your poster still up? Take it down, roll it up and claim the bounty. Where else can a transgressor claim the bounty for their own sins and offenses? Think about this fact! It is well worth it for you to make this choice! Sincerely and with the greatest love, God the Father, Son, and Holy Spirit!

Come to God and cry for mercy. Confess you have been a transgressor and receive Jesus as the substitute for your sins. God wants to say to you; Not Guilty!

If you need to turn yourself in do it now with a humble bow!

4) God is also, the prosecuting attorney that has never lost a case! All have sinned and fall short of the glory of God! (Romans 3:23) The only chance we have is amnesty from God. Thank God for Jesus! He pardons our sins and cleanses us with His imparted righteousness. See 2nd Corinthians 5:21.

5) God in three persons is also the jury in the preliminary hearing of the gospel message. There is a twofold verdict already in place before anything even gets started. One verdict is very good and one verdict is terrible. It depends on the honest confession of the accused person. See Matthew 25: 31-46 (all versions) Take heed! The goat in this passage does not stand for greatest of all time. It stands for God Opposes All Treason!

6) God is the Supreme Court Judge. The Judge of all judges. James 4:12 says there is only One Lawgiver and Judge, the One who is able to save and destroy. Heb.4:13 says this is the God to who we must explain all that we have done. If we could see now what it will be like when we go to the final judgement seat as believers, when all things will already be decided, what would that do to evoke us to obey the gospel fully and carry our witness to the world? If we could watch the judgement of those who reject Jesus Christ right now what would that do to motivate us to the will of God for all people? See John 6:40.

Now, I want to show the wonderful love of God in this message by showing all of you the wonderful differences between Gods Court Room and the courts of the secular world; The courts of men. This can only magnify God's Love for us even more!

1. In the world's courts the truth is not always present because of the weakness of fallen men and women. The innocent can be put in jail and the guilty could be released to go out and do more crime. In Gods court, at the preliminary hearing of the gospel message, truth and justice will always be present for they are attributes of God, Himself.

2. In the world's courts the accused person has no say so to the verdict that the jury will decide. In Gods court, at the preliminary hearing of faith in Jesus Christ, the accused person actually becomes the 4th person of the jury to help decide the

verdict. He or she can help themselves by telling the truth, confessing their guilt, and agreeing with what God says in fact that all our guilty before Him. God will then provide mercy. God's preference is mercy to triumph over judgement. The twofold verdict is always in place. The person's honest response about their sins and their request for mercy will help them to be set free.

3. In the world's court room the accused may be set free and declared not guilty. But, they might leave the court room with only the temporary freedom of this short time on earth. They might not be free of their sins against God; unless they are saved by their correct response to God by the preliminary hearing of faith in Jesus Christ. In God's court room the ones who are set free are free forever with eternal life. We know when the Apostle Paul was in jail he never lost the eternal freedom God gives to all who are truly saved.

4. In the world's court room you can appeal to a higher court some of the time. If an appeal is granted there could be a chance for the verdict to be overturned and the previous decision to be reversed. Time and money will multiply with no guarantee of freedom. In God's court room you have the guarantee of knowing there is no higher court in heaven and earth and it will not cost you any money. It will cost you a sincere and honest confession that you are bankrupt from your sins. We make a humble bow before God asking for forgiveness and the gift of salvation through the appeal Jesus Christ has made to the whole world.

5. This brings us to the next point; the cost financially in the world's court when you appeal to a higher court and you are granted the appeal. People could be spending great amounts of money and owe lawyers for many years. It can be a burden upon burdens and no guarantee of the right and favorable decision of the court. With God's judgement, at the preliminary hearing of faith, the cost is a humble and contrite heart that will bow down to its rightful place before our awesome creator and giver of eternal life. Whosoever will, let him or her drink freely of the water of life! This is the living water. This is life eternal that they may know the Father and the Son whom He sent. (John 17:3)

6. In the world's court room when you are determined not guilty there is no sentence. You are temporarily free to go. In God's court room there is a sentence to be carried out and it takes some Christians a long time to comply. Being freed from sin we became servants of righteousness. (Romans 6:18) We have been given the

ministry of reconciliation. (2nd Corinthians 5:18) We have a debt that can never be paid off. It's a debt to make love payments forever. (Romans 13:8) We are called to the obedience of faith. (Rom. 1:5)

7. The best is for last. In the worlds court room there is no one that is going to take your guilty sentence but you! You're dead! In God's court room there is our very wonderful Mediator who is Courageous, Perfect, Loving, Humble, Holy, Merciful, Kind, Gracious, Wise, Powerful, and Just. He is our Intimate Glorified Servant named Jesus. He took our guilty sentence to the cross as our substitute. He died for our sins and rose from the grave so we could live forever with Him in heaven. Who wants to be an active member of the Highest Court? Who wants to be a real Christian? I will close this message with this event that is coming in our future.

All Rise!

The most High and the most Honorable Judge of the Universe is seated on His Throne!
He is ready to render His Judgement!
Yahweh is present! Jesus the Lamb of God is present!
The Holy Spirit is present! God is fully present!
The Highest Court Room Hearing is now in Session!
The Judgement for all people is to begin now!
Will you be able to stand in this Judgement?

Let us all pray that people everywhere will become Members of the Highest Court calling others to the Hearing of Faith!

Are You A Real Christian

Are you God's vessel and God's vassal
showing victory over hassle?
Are you a repairer of the breach pouring out to someone's reach?
Are you a minister of reconciliation one who brings peace?
Are you an agent of God letting freedom be released?
Are you a servant, a son, a soldier of the king?
Are you abiding in love overcoming evil things?
Are you a member of the highest court calling others to the hearing;
to receive their pardon by confessing their sins
and becoming one who's God-fearing?
Are you living out your sentence as a slave to what's right
with victory over the devil and winning the fight?
Is your allegiance to self or is your allegiance to God?
When the mission is over will you get a well done!
Nod?
Will you look face to face and receive God's open embrace?
From the throne of heaven, will God say, "Christian take your place?"
Are You a Real Christian?

The Hare and the Tortoise

Fable or Reality?

I was self-employed, and one day I felt the Lord tugging me to leave early and go to the library. My work was completed for the day, and there was no work coming until the next day. God was letting me know He had something for me to write, and I needed to get a resource at the library. When I got there, I searched for a fable I had seen a few times when I was growing up. The Hare and the Tortoise. I asked the librarian where I could find it. She said that it was in the children's library. I found it, and I sat down in a small chair and asked God what am I going to do with this? God was going to teach me and show me Christian character through this children's fable.

The race between the speedy hare and the slow tortoise. It starts with the hare mocking the tortoise and making fun of him. The hare boasts about his speed compared to the very slow tortoise. The tortoise was only going to put up with the mocking for a short time. The tortoise challenges the hare to a running race. What was in the mind of the tortoise to challenge such a fast runner? The hare keeps laughing and boasting, believing he could never lose. He accepts the challenge of the tortoise. They find a judge for the race to set the rules and show them the course they have to run. The fox is the wise judge in this fable. The judge will reward the prize to the winner. He tells them the rules to follow before they start. The race is a marathon and not a sprint. It is like the race of faith. Hebrews 12:1-2. NLT says since we are surrounded by a huge crowd of witnesses to life and faith, let us strip off every weight that slows us down, especially the sin that easily hinders our progress. And let us run with endurance the race God has set before us. We do this by keeping our eyes on Jesus, on whom our faith depends from start to finish.) I am going to prove this tortoise is a Christian by the time this race is over.

The fox gets the race started, and off they go. Within a minute or two, the hare is way ahead of the tortoise. The tortoise is going slow but steady. The hare stopped from far ahead and looked back, laughing at the tortoise. He was showing he was prideful, arrogant, and very self-centered in his behavior. How was the tortoise going to beat this arrogant but very talented creature? I noticed that the tortoise was running with his eyes straight in front of him. He was not looking to the left or right and never turned his head to look back. The hare was so far ahead that he decided to take a nap. He fell asleep, and the tortoise kept on going. The tortoise seemed to have a full tank of energy because he had the best pace for a marathon. The tortoise ends up passing the sleeping hare. He just keeps on going slow and steady. When the hare wakes up, he looks back and does not see the tortoise. He looks ahead of him on the course and sees the tortoise is not far from the finish line. The hare sprints as fast as he can to try and catch up. He starts a frantic pace to win, but he comes up short. The tortoise goes over the finish line before the hare! The moral of the story written in the fable is, (Slow and Steady Wins!) But there was a lot more going on in this race besides slow and steady. Reasons for the loss by the hare are more than a few. I will list them so we can all learn why some win in life and why some are big losers.

1. The hare was too proud and pride is a killer. The tortoise never boasted and never mocked the hare. He never retaliated with any wrong behavior. Let's agree the tortoise was showing Christian character. The word of God says the poor in faith can see through the rich one with pride. (Proverbs 28:11.) The tortoise could see the pride and knew a fall was coming to the hare. (Proverbs 16:18) Can we see pride in our self and in others? It is at the root of all sin and the cause of death and all the trouble in the world. Pride is not in God's character. God is always humble. The tortoise who showed humility was the winner over the proud hare.
2. The hare had more natural ability to run than the tortoise did, so the tortoise had to be looking past his own ability to a helper with unlimited ability. He seems to be a Christian even though he is a tortoise!
3. The hare was making comparisons with the tortoise. The tortoise never compared himself to the hare. He was content and secure in who he was and how he was made. He could very well be a Christian even though he is a tortoise!
4. The hare was limited by the conditions of the weather to run the race. He had to have a dry sunny day to get anywhere at all. What am I saying? He needed perfect conditions to run in and the tortoise was prepared to run in all adversity and in any weather conditions. Suppose the rain came pouring down during the race. Suppose the course got flooded with water. The hare would try to take fast little short strokes with those tiny feet instead of the quick jumping strokes that hares can display when they run fast. They can't jump in water or swim very good. The hare would stop and wait for the rain to cease. The tortoise could swim very well because he has the protective shield of his thick shell that can float on the water and he can move very well through the water using the breast stroke of his big wide

legs. The tortoise would gain a big advantage over the hare. It was a tortoise that humans copied the breast stroke from as one of the swimming styles being used!

5. What if there was a hail storm during the race with very little rain? The hare would have to run off the course. He would look for shelter under a tree, a bench or table and wait to proceed like a scared rabbit would. The tortoise would just keep on moving forward with the hail stones bouncing off of his thick protective shell. The attack of his enemy, which in this case is a hail storm, would be resisted and not penetrate his shield so he could keep on running unhindered. His shell was a shield of faith like Christians have. His shield was in a different place than our shield because we don't walk on four legs like he does. He seems to be a real Christian even though he's a tortoise!
6. What if there was a severe snow storm during the race? The course would get ice and snow all over it and the hare would lose his grip and slip and fall. The snow and the ice would prevent him from running. He would be looking for another bench or outdoor table to hide under. Maybe even a parked car or truck would suffice?

On the other hand, the tortoise would have no problems with snow or ice at all. He could jump over on his back and tuck his four legs in to give them a little rest and glide like a saucer sled along the snow and ice. When he slowed down, he could repeat the process. He would still be going at the same pace as his walk, which is slow and steady. He is a good example of what a real Christian would have to face when adversity comes against us.

The weather in the fable was fine, but the tortoise still beat the hare. He had the right pace for the race and was patient and determined to win. He showed character that will always make a winner. I heard a statement one time that being famous is a vapor. Being too popular is an accident waiting to happen. Money and wealth take wings; it says goodbye sooner or later, but character lasts forever! It is the only thing that will last, for it is in the spirit that character is formed. It is not formed in the temporal realm, like being famous, popular, or rich from a financial standpoint. All those things pass away. Character lasts forever! Let's look at the pace and the pattern the hare showed when he lost the race. He was quick to get in front of others.

Do any Christians want to get in front of others? He stopped to sleep. Quick and then stopping; where is the balance in this kind of behavior? He said it was okay to take a break from the race. He became complacent, losing ground with a back-and-forth pattern.

Comparing himself to others, he was saying or thinking wrong thoughts about them. Focused on childish comparisons, he was acting proud and thinking patience is an impossible attitude to have. Does this sound like any Christians would run the race, mocking others, making fun of others, and boasting about their talents to others? The fox set the rules and boundaries for the race, and the hare did not follow them. God sets the rules for our marathon race of faith. We must have a pattern that perseveres and endures while we ask God to give us the character of Jesus to finish the race. God's word says patience in spirit is better than pride. (Eccl.7:8)

God's word tells us to keep our eyes on the finish line, not look to the left or right, and to keep our feet from evil. (Proverbs 4: 25-27)

God, in this fable, did not like the pride the hare showed. In reality, He hated it, but he still loved the hare and gave him the same opportunity to be a winner. There was no evidence the tortoise showed any obvious sins in the race, but we know he had some. He would confess his wrong behavior and always believe and trust in the judge who set the rules. The best quality of the tortoise was his humility. He bowed down to obey and put his trust in the one who had all the ability to make him a winner. The tortoise had great respect for the judge, who had all authority.

When the time came for the judge (the fox or God) to give the reward to the winner, He called both the hare and the tortoise to come forward. The judge was ready to speak and called them to come close to him, face to face. Mr. Tortoise come forward? He obeyed and came close. Mr. Tortoise, did you have any doubt during the race that you could not finish? With half of a smile on his face, the tortoise said, no great and wise judge. I trusted in the helper who is the object of my faith, the judge of heaven and earth who gave us all life. Yes, Mr. Tortoise, you did. Mr. Hare, come forward? Did you have any doubts during the race that you would be unable to finish?

With sweat coming down from his brow and a fearful look on his face, he said, yes, great and wise judge. I did not run the race with faith in you; I only trusted myself. I understand, Mr. Hare. Mr. Tortoise, did you allow any discouragement to come to you during the race? With half of a smile on his face, Mr. Tortoise said, yes, great and wise judge. But I encouraged myself in the promises of the object of my faith who is the judge of heaven and earth and the Lord of my life. When I was far behind, I knew He would bring me to victory. There is nothing too hard for Him, and He gave me the strength to finish. Yes, Mr. Tortoise, I am pleased. Mr. Hare, did you allow discouragement during the race? With sweat coming down from his brow and a fearful look on his face, he said, yes, great and wise judge. I knew I was going to lose because I did not follow your rules, and I did not put my faith in you, great and wise judge. I did not think of praying or talking to the God of heaven and did not believe in anyone but myself. I understand, Mr. Hare. Mr. Tortoise, did you get diverted during the race?

With half of a smile on his face, Mr. Tortoise said, No great and wise judge. Many things could have diverted me, but I stayed on the course, and I was determined to get the prize. I followed Philippians 3:14 in the bible I read. I pressed on toward the goal for the prize of the upward call of God in Jesus Christ.

Yes, Mr. Tortoise, I am pleased. Mr. Hare, did you get diverted during the race?

With sweat coming down from his brow and a fearful look on his face, he said, Yes, I was diverted by my foolish actions and the pride I would not let go of. I refused to trust in the great and wise judge of heaven, who I now know made me and gave me the opportunity to have faith in Him. I was all about me, myself, and I, all of my life. I understand, Mr. Hare. Mr. Tortoise, were you delayed during the race?

With half of a smile on his face, Mr. Tortoise said, yes, there were some delays, but they gave me the patience and determination to persevere in the race. I continued because of the object of my faith. The loving God who made the heavens and the earth and all the living creatures by giving them His breath of life. Yes, Mr. Tortoise, I am pleased. Mr. Hare, did you get delayed during the race?

With sweat coming down from his brow and a fearful look on his face, he said, yes, great and wise judge, I was fully delayed and did not care about following the rules and commands you set. I slept in the bed of my prideful attitude and did not realize my race would end up so bad. I understand, Mr. Hare. You only trusted in yourself. If you had humbled yourself and called on me with remorse, I would have responded with my great love for you. Mr. Tortoise, here is the last question for you to answer.

Were you defeated during the race? With half of a smile on his face, Mr. Tortoise said, No, for the Lord my God, the judge of heaven and earth, gave me the victory when He made me a Christian. The judge had a half of a smile on His face at this response and replied, you are a Christian, Mr. Tortoise? Yes! You know I am. And you know I love you and that I always bow down before your presence in humility, honor, and gratitude and worship You! I am always grateful for Jesus Christ in my life and that He paid the price for all my sins. He died for me so I could live with you, oh, Lord, forever!

Mr. Tortoise, did you ever deny Jesus or deny your faith in Him? I would have died first and never have denied Him! My death would only have been a transfer to my eternal life with the One and Only God! Mr. Tortoise, I take great pleasure in you. Enter into the joy of your salvation and your eternal reward! Well done, good and faithful servant!

Angels of God give Mr. Tortoise an applause that will shake the heavens right now! And they obeyed! From the writer, I hope I have proved that a tortoise can be a Christian! Time for the hare to receive his last question.

Mr. Hare, this is my last question for you. Were you defeated during the race? With much sweat flowing down from his brow and tears piling up in his eyes, he was trembling in fear and having trouble answering the question. He finally answered the great and wise judge, Yes, I was defeated. I did all of life my way listening to Satan's lies. I chose to hate you, the great and wise judge of heaven and earth. I hated you without a cause, for no one could hate you in their right mind.

You were good to me all the time. I was blinded by it. I never thanked you for life, which is a gift that can only come from you! I brought myself to complete defeat. I know now that you are the only God with Jesus Christ and the Holy Spirit. (Silence) for a few moments, then the great and wise judge speaks His final words to the hare. Mr. Hare, I take no pleasure in what I am going to say to you now. Depart from Me! I never knew you! Ref. Matthew 7:23

From the Road with Evil to the Expressway to Heaven Hybrids on the Highway to Heaven!

Will we persevere and endure to the end? We must because our promises are certain in Jesus Christ. We are heading for glory! Don't stop, don't quit make every effort to persevere. We find ourselves in life as a result of the procreation God gave to our human parents. This procreation does go all the way back to Adam and Eve and it's a fact we all should believe. They were the first representatives of the whole human race. We start out on a pathway toward separation from God because in Adam all of us inherited sin. From a spiritual standpoint we all sinned in Adam. Sin was imputed to us. To many of us this seems unfair. All have sinned and fall short of the Glory of God. (Romans 3:23) God has a plan for all to be reconciled to Him through Jesus Christ. God gives us many signs and calls people everywhere as we travel through life. There are three main calls God gives to everyone regardless of where they are located on this earth.

1. God calls people locally by nature. Psalm 19: 1-4 NLT version says, the heavens tell of the glory of God. The skies display His marvelous craftsmanship. Day after day they continue to speak; night after night they make him known. They speak without a sound or word; their voice is silent in the skies; yet their message has gone out to all the earth, and their words to all the world. In Romans 1:20, God has made Himself evident to all men by nature and man is without an excuse to say he does not believe in God.

2. Another way God calls everyone is person to person. Proverbs 20:27 NASB, The spirit of a man is the lamp of the Lord searching all the innermost parts of his being. This means we should all get a signal in our conscience of knowing right from wrong. Our conscience points us to the fact we have a perfect moral Holy God who is always righteous. No matter how hard a person's heart gets you can still make them aware of right and wrong. You can offer them a chair and feed them when they are hungry, and you can take the same chair and hit them over the head with it. God calls us to be sensitive to our conscience and know our spirit is from Him. We are made a spiritual person in God's image and we have not lost everything in

the fall to eliminate our responsibility as his highest creation. We are fallen creatures and responsible persons at the same time.

3. The next way God calls all people is long distance. He sent His only Son to earth on orders from the third heaven! He sent him to die for our sins and to redeem us from eternal death. He takes His long-distance call and conveys it through human messengers so He can give it to every person. He wants everyone to hear it, believe it, and be saved. (John 3:16.) God's long-distance call cost Him the highest price of the sacrifice of His one and only Son. Jesus suffered a double death in our place. He died in His fleshly body and was spiritually separated from the Father for a period of time, suffering eternal death in our place. God sent us an eternal E-Mail when He sent Jesus. Eternal life comes to all who will open the computer of their mind, read and receive God's salvation message and download it to the file of their heart. He wants the message to go to saved mail with everyone. He has sent us His text messages of love and wants us to read all of them. He put them all in the Bible, available to all people. His text messages can also be read at the touch of your fingers on your High Tech cell phones. The Bible is the ultimate book of love. Here is one new acronym for BIBLE—Belonging In Bountiful Love Eternally! We can learn how to live life God's way with God's purpose for us. God can't rewrite the pages of our life if the Bible is closed or not read on our phones. Our lives need to be governed by His book of love so He can recreate us into the image of Jesus Christ. Receive God's text messages every day, and your life will be made new with changes that are necessary. Remember the three calls God gives to all people. Local calls! Person-to-person calls! And one long-distance call to all! Remember your eternal e-mail and read all your text messages. Download everything from God into the file of your heart. Protect your file from any virus trying to attack it and share it with other people who may need it. Now we are going to travel through life together, starting on the road with evil and making a U-turn to the expressway to heaven! We are going to see all the posted signs God gives to direct us to eternal life in heaven. We must put ourselves behind the wheel and travel with perseverance as we see how we become Hybrids on the highway to heaven. As Hybrids, we run on two different kinds of fuel. The world's gas (with a sinful nature) and God's Gas from heaven. G.A S. God's Available Spirit! We start out on the road with evil, as people are separated from God. But God has a different road for us to travel on. (1) The first sign we all see is a Warning sign. We see life is not right, and God warns us about things. A good parent warns their children about the dangers that

exist in life. (2) The second sign we see is a Stop sign. We realize some things should stop. There is sin and evil that needs to stop. (3) The third sign we see is a common information sign; Wrong Way Do not Enter! We concluded from the warning sign and the stop sign that a wrong way was present. But we all have trouble obeying this sign from time to time.

4. The fourth sign we come to is another common information sign. U-turn: this means we can make a 180-degree turn and go in the opposite direction.

5. The fifth sign we see is a yield sign. We are supposed to yield to something or someone in authority. We must submit to someone other than ourselves and stay under authority. The next two signs are crucial! They tell us who that someone is.

6. The sixth sign is another information sign, One Way Only! Jesus! Man's number is six and this sign is vital to life. It is the most important sign men and women can receive. Everyone needs to know there is only One Way God has in mind. There is only one correct way to travel in life! Now, that seems very narrow, doesn't it? You mean I can't go whatever way I want to go? Not if you want to pass out of death into eternal life with God. But you can choose the wide road like many others, but it will lead to eternal death.

7. The seventh sign is the most necessary information sign a person can receive. It leads people to the greatest opportunity in their lives. A chance to be reconciled to their creator. The sign reads, Expressway to Heaven next exit! These scriptures are written on it. Refs. John 14:6, John 3:16, John 5:24.

I'm sure most of us desire to go to a place that is perfect and painless. Heaven surely exists, and Jesus Christ is the only way to get there! We must follow God's information signs 6 and 7 and find the life God intended for everyone. Becoming a Christian starts when we believe sign number 6 and when we take the exit at sign number 7. We make a complete turnaround of 180 degrees. Our destiny is changed by complying with the three ways God calls all people and the correct information signs He gives us on our journey in life. We receive God's mercy and grace, and He promises to direct our new lives in Christ through the Holy Spirit, who He gives to believers. We experience a new freedom and joy of knowing the one and only God! We are now on the expressway to heaven, freely traveling with love and the presence of God with us. It starts out so wonderful, with us enjoying the new way we travel in life, and eventually, we find ourselves in a major traffic jam. Movement on the expressway has come to a crawl. It is not moving at the pace we expect it to. It is not moving at the pace we would desire. Sometimes it comes to a complete stop which makes us idle, and we can't advance at all. We get annoyed and impatient and perplexed. We ask why it may be going so slow. Something or someone else ahead of us must be causing this delay. We assume it has nothing to do with us.

But then we see the number (8) sign. It is another information sign that reads; Under Construction You! What's this all about? I'm under construction? Oh No! We see these scriptures written on it. Philippians 3:20-21 and Romans 12:1-2 I need transformation?

I thought all this was taken care of when I went through the exit to heaven and received God's salvation. No! We have all entered a long construction zone! The pace is very slow, and the number (9) sign is a warning sign. It reads SLOW. We are in a position where we must proceed with caution. While we are crawling along, God points out that we still have some of our old baggage with us. We notice that some of our old clothes are still with us. They are in the case on the front seat. It's not the seat next to us. We are the case that is carrying the old baggage.

We are Hybrids on the highway to heaven. We are now a person of two diverse cultures and traditions. The culture of the fallen world is now in conflict with the culture of God in Christ. A new set of shared attitudes, values, goals, and practices characterize Christ-like living. It is counter cultural to the world's way of living.

God has redeemed us to the truth about life and His intended Will and purpose for mankind. Righteousness is now taking charge over all that is unrighteous. Jesus came to take away the sins of the world. (John 1:29) and (1 John 3:5.) We are to dress ourselves with God's righteousness in Jesus Christ. (Ephesians 4:22-24.)

If we are married or single, traveling alone or with a partner, the old baggage is still with us. We may feel like we have been abandoned, but we are not alone. Here comes a honk from the vehicle next to us! Jesus pulls up next to us in a large U-Haul. This is what is written on the vehicle; JESUS U-HAUL, and under that, it reads ALL OUR BAGGAGE AWAY! He tells us to give Him all our old clothes, which is our sinful nature.

We will be changed into His image by the Holy Spirit He has given us. He wants us to trust in Him to carry us in His love, humility, and holiness. He will carry our old baggage away. We know God is transforming us to enter heaven through His work. We must be patient and persevere in the construction zone. God is with us and helping us to be with Him always. The question is often like this; is God really with us? But the answer that is always with Him is; Yes! I am always with you but are you always with Me? We strive to abide with Him under His direction and authority. Some dangers come our way when we are crawling along on the expressway to heaven. We find we have more time to be distracted by the billboards and ads along the side of the expressway. There are many temptations to our flesh nature to seduce us. Lotto signs tempt us with the love of money. (A stingy man is eager to get rich and is unaware that poverty awaits him. Proverbs 28:22 NIV version.)

There are casino signs tempting us the same way with the love of money. Alcohol signs are being advertised along with nightclubs where men or women can go and see nakedness and even participate in sexual activity if they pay for it. Lust of the flesh signs are in many places. Then, the more deceptive signs only focus on life in this world. They are telling you that enjoyment and pleasure should be your goal and that you can become self-sufficient in all you do. Lying about real success, they only offer the world's definition of temporary success.

The excess of these billboards can become strong temptations to invite us to get off the expressway to heaven and get back on the broad road that leads to destruction. The world and the devil will always try to lure us away from God and His intended will. We should deem it wise not to give in to these temptations, but when we are crawling for a long time, we tend to want to get off and try the old route again. If God would speed up some of these things, I would not be looking at all this stuff! No, not the way it works, men and women of God!

How often have you tried an exit for a while and found out it gets much worse? You want out of the construction zone, and you get anxious and prideful. You're going to do it your own way and have a better time. You may even find it hard to get back on the right course and persevere with the rest of your brothers and sisters. The fast way in this world is going to wear you out, and God will wait until you see clearly He is the Way, the Truth, and the life you need! Look at the wise person in the U-Haul; He is right next to you. He honks his horn again, and you see him pointing the way. Go straight ahead! He is shaking his head; no to the side exits! He is pointing straight, saying no to the left or right turn. Proverbs 4:23-27.

God's endurance and mercy we will always need. We have to remain with God's direction. No wrong exits! We see the number (10) sign. It is a warning that says God's Pace! Whatever it is! He knows the whole picture. He knows there are benefits in going slow. Here is a list of the benefits of God's pace.

1. When we are going slower we can avoid a major crash. Philippians 4:6, Be anxious for nothing. 2 Peter 3:15-patience has a saving effect from God.

2. We can find peace by talking to God and other friends when we are going slower. Be still and know that I am God. (Psalm 46:10) Do all things without grumbling or complaining, (Philippians 2:14) nothing produces more complaining than being is a traffic jam. Put a song on and sing praise to God. Pray for someone. God can be found in the delays of this life.

3. When we are going slower we can recognize when someone else is in trouble on the side of the expressway. When we are not going our normal fast pace we can stop and help someone. When we are moving at a fast pace and in a hurry, we are not going to stop and show love to someone.

4. It is safer to make calls on the expressway when we are in a traffic jam. We can enjoy our friends and be safe if we are crawling along. We can encourage each other and take our attention off the delay. We are eternal beings in the Lord. A moment of patience is nothing compared to the fact that we can never run out of time being the saved people of God. Realize it will always be now for Christians. The Now is eternal! Our Now will never end!

5. Going slow teaches us patience, endurance, perseverance, and flexibility. It helps us in our character to accept that things will not always go the way we want them to. Life is not about us. It really is about God. We exist for Him!

The number (11) sign is another information sign that is a bit encouraging to us. It reads, Construction Ends X Miles Ahead! There is no number written on it but it is telling us it is going to end. How much longer will we be stuck in traffic? The traffic of our personal construction zone?

Then we come to sign (12) it is a duplicate of sign number (6) One Way Only! Jesus! This is to encourage us to press on and never quit. It is a reminder that Jesus is and always will be the only Way! Keep going straight ahead even if it seems the way is narrow. Jesus said it would be narrow. Truth is always narrow. If you make it broad it will deviate from the truth. But some of you are thinking the old road was not that bad. It was moving faster. It has many people who are nice and they are having much fun in their lives. The driver in the U-Haul is coming next to you again. He is pointing straight ahead. No turning back and no side exits your journey is getting close to the end.

Then we see sign (13) an eye opening sign! It even glows in the darkness of night. It says, Eternal life! Paradise with Jesus! Last Exit! Jesus is the light of the world. We are getting close. We are almost home and we will see God! Now I have some questions to ask you.

1. Are you going to stay on the expressway to heaven regardless of the pace of the construction zone? Or are you being drawn to the billboards of earthly life?
2. Are you thinking of making a U-turn back to the old broad road or already in the process of doing it?
3. If you see someone pulled over with their emergency lights flashing are you ready to stop and help? See (Luke 10:25-37) is there any Good Samaritan in you?
4. If you see someone going the wrong direction do you warn them of the danger? Do you honk your horn with the word of God or flash your bright lights with the presence of Jesus in you? Do you help others turn to the Lord?
5. Are you traveling with the highest regard for the safety of others or are you always trying to get ahead of the next person? See Philippians 2: 3-4.
6. Is your life a highway that other people would want to travel on also? Is there someone saying just follow that guy or girl; they know where they are going and what they're doing. Ref. Matthew 5:16, Let your light so shine before others that they may see your good deeds and glorify your Father in heaven. There are many choices to make but we must give priority to one sign. One Way Only! Jesus!
   John 14:6, John 3:16, John 5:24.

We must not forget that Jesus U-Haul is always next to us. We can count on Him to lighten the load. Matthew 11:28-30 NLT Version: (Come to me all of you who are weary and carry heavy burdens, I will give you rest. Take my yoke upon you. Let me teach you, because I am humble and gentle, and you will find rest for your souls. For my yoke fits perfectly, and the burden I give you is light.) We can say to the Lord always, Jesus you haul all our baggage away! We can put on our new robes of righteousness and the new man or woman created in righteousness and holiness of the truth. (Eph. 4: 22-24.) For the Christians who are a bit sophisticated they can give a paraphrase for this verse. They can Doff their Dirty Dapple and Don their Devine Dazzle! For Christians who are creative in their speech we can say-- We are no longer a Chip off the old Block, but a Permanent Part of the Real Rock's Flock!

Here is the final advice for Hybrids on the Highway to Heaven

1. Focus straight ahead don't turn left or right turn from evil. Prov. 4:27
2. Focus on the One Way Only! Jesus! John 14:6, John 3:16, John 5:24
3. Trust in God and we will never run out of Gas or Provision! Phil.4:13, 19
4. We must maintain our maintenance programs! 2: Peter 1:3-8
5. Keep your headlights working at all times! 1 Cor. 2:16, John 8:12. We have the mind of Christ and the Light of the world!
6. We will have to travel through some bad storms! Matthew 7:24-25, I Corinthians 3:11-Our solid foundation is Jesus the Rock! We build our lives on Faith in Him!
7. Get your washes on a regular basis! Read and Do the Word of God! James 1:21-22- Be Doers of the Word!
8. Keep your wipers working at all times! 2 Cor 4:4, 1 Peter 5:8, the god of this world wants to blind people from the truth and kill them!
9. Keep a shining appearance and a glow of protection every day. Solitude with God! Luke 5:16, Luke 6:12, Matt 14:23. We are every day Christians!
10. Stay tuned up so you always have a reserve of power. 1 Thess. 5:17 Always Pray! It's on an off all day meaning you are ready at any time.
11. Stay filled with God's Gas from heaven! G.A.S. God's Available Spirit! Ephesians 5:18, Zech 4:6 (It is by His Spirit)
12. Don't Quit! Persevere with God! Matt. 24:13, Rom 2:7, Heb. 6: 11-12, Rom 5:3-5, James 1:4, Rom 8:37-39 and lastly Rev 3:21 Endure, Overcome, Obey, Give thanks! See all these references in all versions of God's Word.

Captain God wants First Mates to handle His fishing Business!

Mathew 4:19 All Refs. Follow Me and I will make you fishers of men. God has a Five Step Fishing Process for Christians to Carry Out.

1. Find the men God's fishing for.
2. Catch the men God's fishing for.
3. Clean the men God has caught fishing
4. Prepare the men God has caught fishing
5. Serve the men God has prepared back to the world. (Always inclusive for all women also)

What does it mean to be a first mate?

1. Companion and assistant to a more skilled worker
2. A deck officer on a merchant ship ranking below the Captain
3. A matched couple-one of a pair.

The first two answers are what we will be focused on. The last one does not apply to this message. Captain God has no equal correspondents among men or angels. In fact, that is what started all the trouble; a rebellion to be equal with God. Christians are companions to the most skilled worker of all; God Himself. We rank under Him to obey His perfect authority. Captain God has a large fishing business to operate. We are His first mates. God's fishing merchandise is of the highest quality. God paid the highest price for His merchandise. As fishers of men, the goal is to make people the disciples of Jesus our Lord. God says we have been bought with a price.

The price was the shed blood of Jesus dying in our place. See 1 Peter 1:18-19 Ref. We have been sought by God, caught by God, bought by God, and brought to God to be cleaned, prepared, and served back to the world. To save the lost people in this world, we are to give them the food that does not perish. See John 6:27 (Reference). God wants fishers of men to produce more fishers of men. He prays for all that He has purchased by His redemption to share in the fishing process with others after they are cleaned, prepared, and given His commission to take His gracious plan to others.

Step one is finding the people. Scriptures that apply for reference are Luke 19:1-10, Matthew 28:19-20, Romans 10:14-17, John 6:40. We do God's will when we search to find the lost and to show and tell them the gospel through deeds of love and speaking God's Words of Truth.

Step One: What are some of the ways we can find the lost? If you turn on your human fish finder, it will start beeping or giving a signal as soon as you walk through your local neighborhood. Every street you go down or travel on is full of people God wants to find, catch, and save into His kingdom. Open your spiritual eyes and ask God to give you the right plan to love others. He will help you use the right words to tell them about your faith which is real because of the reconciliation that has taken place. He is the only God, and no other religion can say they have reconciled to the false gods they may believe in. They certainly know they are not reconciled within themselves. Their false faith does not go past their thinking to a real experience in a changed heart. We must sow seeds of love and make love payments in all the little things that speak the gospel very loudly. Pray God will draw people to His reconciliation through Jesus Christ. People associated with the Christian church have heard that Jesus died for all sins and forgave them. But forgiveness does not become real until reconciliation is established. They must be humble and ask for the salvation of God, knowing they desperately need it. If you have the courage to be an intentional witness for God, you can visit places like nursing homes and hospitals and visit people who may be alone. They may welcome you as a friend because they cannot live a normal life confined to their circumstances. They will often be happy you came to visit them, and not ask you to leave. Always pray first, and you will see what a pleasure it is to watch God Work.

Step Two: (Catching the people) Start with the knowledge of the truth by knowing the word of God regarding the presentation of His message, the proclamation of the word with the help of the Holy Spirit, who is the exclusive messenger. The gospel speaks for itself and proves itself to be true. It draws others because God is always talking through it. We are empty vessels and channels for the Spirit to use. I believe all Christians can know the basics of the gospel message and tell others about it. There are at least three salvation verses in John and three in Romans that are very good for letting others know how much God loves them and wants them to be saved. We represent the triune witness of God. The words of the Spirit give proclamation. It is also essential to practice the good deeds of love from the Father whenever we witness. People knowing you care for them will give validity to God's love. In John 14:10-11 NASB, Jesus told those who doubted his words to believe Him by the deeds they saw him doing. We can find time to give a helping hand to others when they need it. We can also give the little things that mean a lot. We can give to the poor because of what God gave to us. Dividing your bread with those who have very little and making love payments on a continual basis. See Romans 13:8. It tells us we owe love to all people because of the great love God has shown us. Our interest level should be going up in making more love payments! This is one place where a higher interest level is always good. We can give love to people who may be acting like our enemy or proving to be one. By blessing this person instead of ignoring them or retaliating in our flesh nature toward them, we could convict them to see the depth of God's great love for them. We also show the witness of God with the character of Christ, who is in us by the Spirit. Gentle and kind and patient in our attitudes show them the nature of Jesus. Being humble and not boasting shows them Jesus. Forgiving small things very quickly or gently confronting people with the right words to reconcile any differences will keep the peace and build intimacy with them, showing the character of Jesus. We can regard others as more important than ourselves to bring a balance showing we are not self-centered on our own interests. Ref. Phil. 2: 3-4. We can know God has given all people great value, and we can go past all the dirt to bring out the treasure in other people. Digging for lost treasure requires people to get past the dirt first. Seeing people as God sees them is knowing God wants them covered by the blood of Jesus and saved into His kingdom. He died for ALL! Let your gentle disposition and your confident body language do the speaking for you when you are silent. Radiate the sweet fragrance of Jesus, for that is what we are doing for the ones who will come to God. 2 Corinthians 2:15-16. An important thing to know is when we are fishing for souls to come to God, we fish with a net! Not Hooks! There is deception in using a hook. Witnessing for God never uses deception, only the truth. When a fish hook is covered, it snares and pierces the fish it catches. When a person is drawn into God's net, they get rescued from the world's polluted waters and stop swimming their old way. The net does not harm the person. The net allows the Holy Spirit to create the current to guide the person to salvation. Jesus said we are to draw all men to Him. The disciples never ripped their catch apart or hit them over the head, trying to catch them. What's your fishing technique? Some of you may need to dock your motor boats and maybe your motor mouths and stop making waves. Proverbs 19:2 (NIV) says it is not good to have zeal without knowledge, nor to be hasty and miss the way. You can miss the way with your witness or chase people away if you fish without knowledge. Draw people to Jesus. God tells us when and where to drop our nets. Tune in to the Holy Spirit, who knows the end from the beginning. Learn to be skilled fishermen. We must be smooth operators, bold but very gentle, and assertive but patient. If you're always using a hook or an aggressive style, remember getting hooked on something generally implies an ignorance from the person's choice more than a willful acceptance. The devil uses a hook in this world to steal, kill, and destroy. We often hear stories about how a person got hooked on drugs or alcohol. A hook is synonymous with a snare or a trap. All of them are saying pain is coming. But the net says relief has arrived after it pulls the person to safety in the kingdom of heaven! The Holy Spirit guides the people into a safety net where they will not get hurt. They get rescued and brought back to God. We need to fish God's way with compassion for every lost person in the polluted and poisonous waters of the world. The last point on catching the people is to keep your nets in the water and never stop fishing, regardless of the outcome. God says to give them the gospel, and He knows who will and will not receive it. Have the word of God ready on your tongue, and keep reaching out with love and good deeds. Most lost people are not aware that they need a safety net and a rescue from the world. They are looking to fill their mouths and appetites with what the world offers. We must divert them to the real food that does not perish. The food of eternal life. Ref. John 6:26-27. After we give them the food they are used to, we can let them know there is an eternal food waiting for them to partake of. This is why we must feed the poor regularly. They are much more open to being rescued than the ones who have the riches of the world. Red, Brown, Yellow, Black, and White, everyone can get a metaphysical bite of the food that does not perish!

Step Three: (The cleaning of the people.) How do we clean them? We teach them the bible and teach them to pray. We guide them to a good bible-based church and get them into fellowship with their new brothers and sisters in Christ. We encourage them to spend time with God as they start each day. Alone with God before they go out into this world for another busy day. References for cleaning scriptures are 2 Timothy: 2:15, 1 Thess. 5:17, John 17:17, Matt. 20: 25-28, John 14:23, 1 John1:7. We can practice these and grow in our sanctification.

Step Four: It is imperative to spend time in solitude. Why? It gives us genuine intimacy with God. This is where the baking and broiling part really comes in. Sitting with God alone provides the most important part of the cleaning process. A direct condescension occurs! He will meet you when you sit at His feet. He will manifest His presence since He is always there with you. Under His authority, you can receive His personal tangible love! You get fresh food for you to chew and digest. He delights in His personal feeding by the Holy Spirit, who cleans your spirit and body with the washing of the water of the His word. He works to refine us from the inside. He brings this to us when we spend time alone in solitude. We are being prepared the way the Captain has designated. Learning from pastors and teachers and evangelists, and all the ones who equip others, is very important. But, and I do mean but, just learning from them will not get the baking and broiling done! You have to sit in the Refiner's fire. He has to bake and broil every impurity out as we go through sanctification. Some people only go to secondary sources and avoid their primary source, which is God alone. They find it easier because of the equal correspondence. Do you depend on pastors and teachers for all your growth? The highest power and the greatest personal relationship in the universe may seem intimidating to those who are not availing themselves to the change that is necessary by the Holy Spirit. There could be some pride or ignorance keeping them back, but if they seek Him one-on-one, they will see His gentle presence and fall more deeply in love with the giver of life. The conviction He brings when we make the time for Him convinces us tenderly and does not intimidate us. Times of laughter will not be absent when you experience God's sense of humor at times when you may not be looking for it. You may end up crying tears of joy and tears of gratitude. Realize the privilege it is to sit in the presence of God, and you will want the Holy Spirit to teach you more. He does more than teach us. He transforms us into the image of Christ. He is our greatest love and our protection from evil. He is our helper and our guide. He has a role that not too many realize. He is our truant officer! If you stop going to school trying to play hooky, He will always come after you in a loving way. He is God the Holy Spirit conveying all the Son has given us. He hears from the Father and the Son and gives it to us. (1 John 2:27) He also intercedes for us with a perfect prayer to the Father and the Son. (Romans 8:26) See the poem in Section Three called Face to Face in Fellowship God's with me God's here! Revelation 3:19-22 NASB, says Behold, I stand at the door and knock; if anyone opens the door, I will come in to him and will dine with him and he with me. He who overcomes, I will grant to him to sit down with me on my throne, as I also overcame and sat down with my Father on His throne. He who has an ear, let him hear what the Spirit says to the churches). And what the Spirit says to each one of the church body when they sit alone with God in solitude! We can realize the intimacy God wants to have with us. It is amazing love and the greatest privilege in life as we know it.

Step Five: Serving the people God has saved back to the world. Romans 6:18 NLT says, Now you are free from sin, your old master, and you have become slaves to your new master, righteousness. (Past tense) We find the word slaves in more than one version because God has purchased His church with His shed blood to bring His righteousness to the world. Every salvation is the imputation of God's righteousness which can only come in Jesus Christ. One wonderful verse in 2nd Corinthians 5:21 Ref. We exchanged our sins for His righteousness and got such a deal! We are called to feed the world with the truth of eternal life. We are the righteousness of God in Christ, the hope of glory! The common ministry we all have as saved children of God is the ministry of reconciliation. When we all know our gifts from God, we all contribute to this common goal. Our personal gifts from the Holy Spirit employ us in Captain God's five-step fishing process. All Christians are in unity as the crew under Captain God's authority, and we serve one another in love for each other. This is seen by the people we are going to catch. Ref. John 13:35. We were not sought, caught, bought, and brought to God to be served, but to serve others and give our life for others.

The five-step process under Captain God's control brings eternal life and sanctification to all who are part of the church and all who will become part of the church. The greatest in the kingdom will be a servant to all. (Matthew 23:11.) It started with Jesus, the suffering servant who became the glorified servant. Our greatness can only come from being a servant of God and serving all people with His love.

Now, I want to draw an important comparison between Captain God's five-step fishing process and the world's way of fishing through man's own religion and his false effort to find the way to God. The world has a three-step plan. They find some people looking to acknowledge there is a God. They catch some of them, and then they put them on ice! It is what the real fish markets do. Stay with me, and I will explain this point. In the world's fish markets, the fish are found, caught, brought to the market, and put on ice to be sold to the people. This allows the people to pick and choose what they think is right about how to clean and prepare them. Religion in the world does the same thing.

Being on ice indicates that the object or food is waiting to be cleaned, prepared, and served from a feeding process. All the false religions, including a false representation of Christianity, are a result of people who are not reconciled to Jesus Christ. They will practice the traditions of men and women and make an effort to please God from the works of the flesh or the laws they all know are present. By the works of the flesh or the law, no person will be justified. They will not become the righteousness of Jesus Christ Ref.

Romans 3:20. People might believe they can please God to His appeasement or satisfaction. By not being reconciled to the one and only God, they will not abide in His instructions. They would not have the active indwelling of the Holy Spirit to sanctify and conform them to the image of Jesus Christ. Their religion would be relative to their own way of thinking. Is God a higher power only? Is God going to accept me if I have good morals and do good things? Will I get to heaven if it really exists?

The world's three-step process leads them to deception. It leaves God's process of cleaning, preparing, and serving, out of His control in their lives. They are left with their own ways of thinking. It evokes the flesh nature and the prideful spirit of people who do things their own way. They end up under the power of the evil one unless Jesus Christ sets them free. Ref. 1 John 5:19. There is only one way to God! Ref. John 14:6. Salvation is much more than just a catch! What if the disciples had stopped the process after they found the people and caught them with the gospel net? They would have been disobedient to the full command in Matthew 28:19-20.

God's way has Him dictating and commanding the cleaning, preparing, and serving process after we have found and caught the people with His great salvation. We follow the whole process, so the meal or the food we give to others is the food that does not perish. The food that leads to eternal life is the most important food that we can work for. John 6:27 tells us the Father sent Jesus to give us the spiritual food of the gospel message to receive eternal life. The main difference is that the world only markets the temporary. All the people have relative beliefs, and let's hope there is an afterlife for us. God has a free market for eternal life. The world has a common philosophy: I do it my own way. It leads to death, Refs. Proverbs 14:12. All false religions are under this evil and wrong mindset. They can find some people and tell them they have a way to God. The bottom line is that they find people, catch them, and put them on ice. By the way, are some Christians acting like the frozen chosen? Are any of you real Christians sitting on ice right now? God did not put you on ice. You put yourself there when you don't cooperate with His fishing process.

I have had some chilling experiences myself. Is there a need for any of you to thaw out? Do you need to be seasoned with salt? Do you need to get the sweet spices of Jesus so you can be a fragrance of life to others? Do you need some fire to bake and broil the impurities out? Get back in the Refiner's fire! Get back to the word of God and prayer and obey being a doer of the word. Start serving someone other than yourself. Sit at the feet of Jesus under His authority and receive His power and love. Bow down to His mercy and grace.

Some of us may have been on ice so long that we could only make a good meal for a Polar bear! Who else could eat an ice-cold fish? Ahoy Mate! This is your Captain speaking! How's my fishing business doing, Mate? How much time are you putting in, Mate? Where's your next catch, Mate? Are you building more cleaning facilities, Mate? How are your preparations going, Mate? Are you using the right seasoning and being the salt of the earth, Mate? I'm ready to bake and broil, Mate! Do you have a new supply for Me, Mate? If you love Me, you will obey Me! Follow Me! First mates! I have made you fishers of men! Never forget when you were sought, caught, bought, and brought to Me! I preached you in! I will teach you in! I will forever keep you in! Now is the time of salvation, Mate! Ship Ahoy Mate! Acclamation to the Captain! There is something to gladly cheer about!

Success in the Highest Way Possible!

What is real success, and what does it mean to succeed in life? Webster tells us the definition of success and succeed. We have small levels of success and succeed in small ways, and we would all like to have great success and succeed in much bigger ways. In our life, failure is never a welcomed option to end up with. Most people would give the world's definition of success before the very best and highest definition. This is only because most people don't think with an eternal perspective. We will start by looking at Webster's definition—A degree or measure of succeeding, having the most favorable outcome. This is the primary definition. The secondary definition is the attainment of wealth, favor, or eminence. This kind of success is temporary and can only last for a limited time. Would it not be much better to have success that can never end? Success that will last forever? Yes, it most definitely would be better. Eternal success sounds fitting to everyone because it indicates there would be no death. Life after death is a fact in Jesus Christ. He is the eternal God, and He offers eternal life to all who will place their trust in Him and humbly bow before their God, who gave them life. He was raised from the dead and wants to raise us to eternal success with everlasting life. Let's look at some small successes most of us have in life. We can make a list.

1. The child learns to walk after crawling. This becomes a small success.
2. The child learns to ride a bike. This becomes a small success.
3. The child studies and gets a good report on learning. Another small success.
4. The teenager gets his first job and earns money. A small success.
5. The child graduates from college and gets a good paying job. A larger success but still temporary and not the best success in life.
6. The man gets married to a good woman and has a beautiful family. The family stays together. This is a big success because relationships are critical in life. Money can't buy love!
7. This family has come to a point where they feel like they're on top of the world. Worldly success is theirs. But life seems to be going too fast and it is getting much tougher to keep up with everything. Something about this kind of success, seems to be vanity and is meaningless.

No one is really happy, and no one is satisfied anymore. Problems seem to be everywhere. This success seems to be missing something. In their hearts, they are not happy. What is missing inside them? Their souls are hungry for more. The answer won't be found in what's missing. It is found in WHO is missing. The highest success can only be found in the primary definition of the most favorable outcome! The most favorable outcome can only result in their awareness of the truth. They want to live forever in peace and contentment with no sorrow or pain. They need to know their Creator. He surely lives for eternity and has been put into the hearts of all people. Many people ask: Will I die thinking this was all there is about life? There has to be more, or it makes no sense. What is success if we have to die and leave the life of the living? But some people believe it ends on earth, and they do everything they can to hang on to it. They believe in the lie about the definition of worldly success, attainment of wealth or eminence only. They did not grasp the real definition of worldly success from God's standpoint. It is in this acronym the Lord gave to me. The acronym comes from the actual word itself. God's definition of the world's SUCCESS equals:

Secular Undertakings Can't Carry Eternal Salvation Status.

It can only be temporary! It makes the suggestion there is nothing else. People might think they're all going into the ground to be no more! So get all you can as long as you can do it. They have lived their life on the lie of a temporary status only. They rejected the reality that God put eternity into the hearts of men; Eccl. 3: 11 NIV. In ignorance, men and women reject the message of the living God and the gospel of Jesus Christ. We are all made eternal beings, and it is only a question of where will we spend eternity after the first death. How do we get to the highest definition of success?

Having the most favorable outcome! The answer is found in Romans 6:22. Regarding Christians-- but now, having been freed from sin and enslaved to God, you derive your benefit, resulting in sanctification and the outcome: eternal life. NASB. Some versions will say- result in eternal life. The result is the same as the outcome in any circumstance. This brings us to the way we get the most favorable outcome or result. It is also an acronym God gave to me. The acronym comes from the actual word itself once again.

SUCCESS—Submission Under Christ's Control Extracting Self Sufficiency.

A person must die to controlling their own life and give it to God because of His great love and promise to us. What could be a better outcome or result than living forever with God? God will raise us from the first death to the eternity that was always intended for us. We never fear what can kill the body and what can't kill our soul. (Matt.10:28) We are safe with Him forever! You will see there are two key words to receive the Lordship of Jesus in our lives. They are Submission and Humility. We must drop all pride and completely depend on God to control our lives with the sanctification from being born from above. Real success is waiting for all people, and God wants everyone saved to eternal life. Keep your trust in Him always, for this world is not our eternal home. Tell others how to be successful and show them the way. I want to share more acronyms from all the words that are about our success from God. The first one is to succeed. We will succeed and follow after Christ when we gain our inheritance from Him.

1. Succeed --- Submission under Christ's control entering eternal destiny
2. Successful—Submission under Christ's control extracting self-sufficiency finding unfailing love.
3. Successor—Submission under Christ's control extracting self-sufficiency obtaining Righteousness
4. Submission---Staying under by much intended spiritual strength in our nature---(The nature of Jesus when He is in us.) Here are some scriptures that refer to our inheritance in Christ. We have to look at Webster's definition on the word succeed first. It brings things together in a convincing manner. Succeed is to come next after another in office or position or in possession of an estate-especially to inherit sovereignty rank or title. <u>To follow after another in order to turn out well.</u> To attain to a desired object or end. To pass to a person by inheritance- to follow in sequence—immediately to come after as heir or successor. Look at the confirmation God gives us from His word in regard to our inheritance in Christ.

Ephesians 1:18- We receive the riches of the glory of His inheritance in the Saints—we will succeed and gain the inheritance of God.

1 Peter 1: 3-4- We obtain an inheritance which is imperishable and undefiled and will not fade away! It's eternal and undefiled. (No Sin)

Titus 3:7- We are justified by grace and we are made heirs according to the hope of eternal life.

Colossians 1:12- Our heavenly Father has qualified us to share in the inheritance of the Saints in light. (And who is the light of the world? Jesus!) Through the Lord Jesus we will approach the unapproachable light and we will see God! The beginning and the forever! The never ending perfect life without pain and sorrow! Wow! What a blessing! Jesus has prepared a place for us to be with Him forever!

(John 14:2-3) Jesus said I will come again and receive you to Myself, that where I am you may be also. He is permitting us to live forever with Him! Bow down with gratitude and worship Him. We will be complete in love and wisdom and power. It is beyond what we could ever hope for.

See 2nd Corinthians 3:5 as it reminds us where all our sufficiency is. Our sufficiency is from God. We could never be adequate or sufficient apart from Him. See Job 34:14, Isiah 42:5, and Acts 17:24-25 they remind us of our complete dependency upon God to breathe the breath of life every minute. Refer to the principles from these next verses of scripture.

Colossians 3:24, Think with eternity in mind and set your minds on things above!

Joshua 1:8, do according to what is written in God's Word and you will have good success. Submit and obey and live out the privilege of knowing God and making Him known to others.

See Romans 8:1-4, The Law of the Spirit enables us to obey God. We walk according to the Spirit. See Romans 5:5, The Holy Spirit has given us a full pouring out of God's love to live in submission to Him and share His love with others. We can obey and be blessed with the highest success. Pray for all the Saints who will succeed and follow after Christ and for all the people with the temporary success of the world to find the highest success possible. Eternal life is in Jesus Christ alone! Amen!

The Best is for Last when the world's in your Past!

It's time to Refine and be filled with New Wine! (John 2:1-11.)

There is a wedding taking place in Cana of Galilee. This wedding will include a resurrection miracle as we take a deep look at this text. The Son of God brings transformation power, which is what His mission is about. We are going to see that salvation is always His objective. Verse three tells us the wine had run out. The time of celebration was about to be interrupted. This would have been a very embarrassing situation for the groom who was getting married. It was a custom for the groom to plan all the necessary arrangements for a wedding that usually lasted as a weeklong celebration. They have no more wine. It sounds like the party is over. They are all running dry. Mary is asking Jesus to do something about the situation. Jesus responds to her that his time has not yet come. Jesus was referring to a time when the Father would glorify the Son by His death and resurrection to save the world in John 17.

What Mary was asking Jesus was going to become a preview of God's supernatural power of transformation. Jesus also reminds her that He is under His heavenly Father's highest authority. Mary's request was indirectly calling for a miracle. She put a demand of God's anointing on Jesus, and He will come through! Mary speaks to the disciples the wisest words she could ever speak;

Whatever HE says, Do It! Hearing this statement, the best focus is on who is saying it above and beyond what is said. When the disciples know God is talking, they carry out the request He is asking them. Jesus is not an ordinary man! We should all start with this in mind regarding all of Jesus's commands.

Psalm 119:30 NIV. I have chosen the way of truth; I have set my heart on your commands. This is a good start.

John 2:5 is good for all the in-betweens. Do what He says!

Psalm 119:44 NIV says I will always obey your law forever and ever! This would be the perfect ending. Let's move to verse six in this text. Six water jars are used by the Pharisees for ceremonial washing, each holding twenty to thirty gallons. Jesus says to fill the jars to the brim! We have 120-150 gallons of water at this point. There are several insights to draw from this verse. God is getting ready to bring some truth over the hypocritical practices of the Jewish Pharisees. They used these water pots for ceremonial washing. They would wash their hands from things they touched during the day that they believed were unclean. The pots cleaned the dirt on the outside, not the dirt or sin inside of all people. They practiced the letter of the law but not the spirit of the law. Jesus tells the disciples to draw some of the water out of the jars and take it to the master of the banquet. Jesus turned the water into wine, but He showed us much more. The bible says man's number is six. There are six stone jars. In Genesis, God formed man out of the dust of the earth, and this included things in the earth's makeup. Clay is sometimes used in the bible to describe people. God is the potter, and we are the clay.

There is also a key verse in Ezekiel 36:26. NASB. I will give you a new heart and put a new spirit in you. I will remove from you your heart of stone and give you a heart of flesh. We are talking about six stone water pots here in John. We could say we are made like the stone water pots. What is the difference between stone and dust? Stone is hard, and dust is soft. God made man from the dust. We all started out with soft material. The water pots have the same makeup as people. They started out soft and got hard over time. We also know that when the body dies, it returns to dust.

The reason for hardness is described in the bible as sin. A hard-hearted man is equivalent to a man with sin. That is why God says He wants to remove the heart of stone and give us a heart of flesh. Here the heart of flesh means an obedient heart. A heart before it is hardened with sin. A hard heart is no longer pliable, and God wants a soft heart to work with, an obedient heart.

The next insight from this verse is that the six jars are filled to the brim with water. People are filled with water. Our first birth is called the water birth. The body is 60 percent water. The muscles are 75 percent water. The blood is 82 percent water. The bones are 25 percent water. The six stone pots can, in many ways, represent the first creation in Adam. We are born like water pots from the makeup God used and the sin nature we inherited in Adam. We are hardened from sin. Jesus told the disciples to draw the water out and turned it into wine.

There are more insights here. Man needs to have his water birth turned into the new wine of God's salvation. John 3: 3, 5, 7 says man must be born again of the spirit, which is referred to as new wine in the scripture. Transformation is being demonstrated, and the water to wine indicates that men will be transformed and made new by the spiritual birth we all must receive! The new wine refers to the Holy Spirit, who gives us regeneration and new birth in God's resurrection life. Titus 3:4-7 NASB. This is a complete sign and the foreshadowing of the great commission where Jesus tells the disciples to go into the world and reproduce the salvation process. This will change men and women from their water birth to the new wine of the Spirit and regenerate the souls of all who will believe! Jesus is saying if He is lifted up, He will draw all men and women to himself. Drawing people from the first Adam with the hard sinful nature to the Second Adam, Jesus, who gives the Holy Spirit, which is the new wine of Spiritual life. Jesus tells the disciples to take the water turned to wine to the head waiter.

The head waiter already knows the best wine was given first, and the watered-down wine was used last before it ran out. This man is about to get a new taste of the new wine in more ways than one; the best quality possible. The head waiter does not know where the new wine came from. John 3:8 says we don't know where the wind comes from or where it is going, and so is everyone who is born of the spirit. This means we can't fully explain it, for it reaches past our understanding into the supernatural realm of God! God's salvation is also seen in the amount of wine that Jesus produced from the six stone water pots. Each water pot was twenty to thirty gallons. When they started the wedding, the wine was in wineskins and then put in bottles placed on the tables. They would drink, celebrate, and ask for more bottles to be brought to the tables. We now have one hundred and fifty gallons of new wine to drink. Jesus would not say fill them to the brim if he did not intend on changing all the water to wine. Jesus made the equivalent of four or five bathtubs full of new wine. More than the people can consume, especially at this point in the wedding celebration. Ref. Ephesians 3:20 says Our God is able to do more than we could ask or think of by His power.

They will have wine left over. God is a God of more than enough! Moving to verse nine in this text, it says the disciples knew where the new wine came from. They knew Jesus was doing a miracle. Here is where this wedding gets really good. Lord Jesus, put us into this wedding in our imaginations. Open our minds to hear what you are about to show us. The head waiter is overwhelmed by the new wine. He calls for the bridegroom to come to him. We are going to use more of God's truth here, even though it's not directly in this text. I felt deeply inspired by the Lord to write this. It brings out more deep insight into the power of Jesus and what he will do through the scriptures regarding His true mission.

The bride and the bridegroom are sitting together. They're making a toast with their glasses, and maybe he is already nibbling on her neck. He is unaware the wine has run out. After all, he is not responsible for the new supply, is he? Jesus is the one who made the new supply. The head waiter signals the bridegroom to come over and explain the new wine to him. The bridegroom says to the bride-to-be, Honey, I will be back in a few minutes and starts to walk toward the head waiter. When he gets halfway there, Jesus meets him in the middle of the room! Jesus speaks, be still, son! The bridegroom looks into the eyes of the

Son of God standing right in front of him. Yes, master Jesus what is it you want? Jesus tells him the situation. You allowed the wine to run out. You did not plan carefully, and you were responsible for meeting all the requirements of the wedding with enough wine. But I will not let you be shamed by your guests, for you know the customs and how the Jews live up to them. I am going to spare you from the shame and ridicule. I have carried the responsibility for you and covered all your inadequacies. I have supplied the wedding with an abundance of new wine. The bridegroom bows down to Jesus and thanks him from his heart. Jesus tells him to go back to his bride and that God will get involved with them on their honeymoon.

And now the real bridegroom has appeared! I said the real bridegroom has appeared! (Matthew 9:15) The real bridegroom walks over to the head waiter. Jesus is the only one that can explain the new wine. It only comes from Him. Jesus approaches the head waiter. The headwaiter looks into the eyes of God, who is one with Jesus! He knows Jesus is standing and speaking in the place of the bridegroom, who is getting married in the natural human tradition.

Our substitute and our mediator between all men and God is going to make Himself known to the headwaiter. Jesus comes to him as our mediator to deal with the facts in complete truth. Jesus tells the head waiter that He is the one who produced the new wine. The headwaiter looks closer into the eyes of the one who is fully man and fully God! The head waiter says men bring their choice wine out first, and after the people have drunk freely, the cheaper wine is brought out. But you have saved the best for last. The headwaiter knows Jesus is not like other men.

Now suppose Jesus had a conversation that lasted longer with this headwaiter. Imagine this is what it was. Jesus asks this headwaiter, "Do you see the deception you are practicing here?" This is the way of man apart from God. You know they have drunk freely, and hope they do not recognize when the cheaper wine comes out. You do this so you can make more profit for yourself. You are relying on delusion! The world offers a watered-down version of life. It can start out good, but it gets worse over time and leads to destruction. The world can only be temporary in what it offers to people.

God offers eternal satisfaction in everlasting life that does not fade or get deluded. He always offers the best for last for those who put their trust in Him. The head waiter is getting much conviction at this point. Jesus tells him that He did not come to condemn him but to save him. Jesus continues with two questions. Do you want to receive this new wine permanently? Do you want to live forever with God? Knowing his sins fully, the head waiter embraces Jesus and bows down to Him. Yes, master, I confess I have done deception, and I ask forgiveness for my sin. I receive you with gratitude, and I will serve you in faith. From now on, I will only be a new wine promoter. Jesus speaks with thanks to His Father and the Holy Spirit. This is the concluding statement of the miracle at the wedding.

Here is a list of the results that <u>could have occurred</u> at this wedding: The original bridegroom could have gotten married twice. Once to his wife and then to Jesus. He could have received Jesus. The head waiter could have been converted from deceiving people, from his avaricious gain, to become a new wine promoter for the Kingdom of God in Christ! The disciples could have learned their call earlier than they did to draw people out of their sinful water birth and lead them to the Salvation of the new wine in Jesus Christ. The Holy Spirit will be regenerating the hearts of many with eternal life! (Titus 3:4-7). Isiah 25:6 NIV says- (On the mountain of God) the Lord Almighty will prepare a feast of rich food for all peoples, a banquet of aged wine--the best meats and the finest of wines. Many have said that wine gets better with age. This is true if you're referring to time as we know it. But there is a Wine that is not subject to time. It is before all time and will be after all time. New wine from the Holy Spirit excels over any wine because it has existed and will exist for all of eternity. The new wine Jesus has to offer all people is eternal life! The Best is for Last when the worlds in your Past! It's time to Refine and be filled with NEW WINE!

The Host, the Baker, the Grill Man and the Waiter!

The 21st Chapter of John has been taught and preached often over the years. The miracle of the 153 large fish and the meeting Jesus has with Peter, which many call the three love confessions to encourage Peter. I believe there is a very good message to teach from verses 9-14. Let's try to put ourselves in the situation as it was happening. It is early in the morning, and the sun is just starting to rise. It is at the Sea of Tiberias on the west shore of Galilee. The seven disciples who were fishing see Jesus standing on the shoreline, but at this point, they are not sure who it is. This is the third time Jesus appears after the resurrection. Remember this fact; AFTER the resurrection. The Glorified Jesus is in His glorified body. This means He has finished the work the Father sent Him to do, saving the world from their sins and bringing redemption to all who will believe in Him. He shed His blood for all, and the mission was complete. The way to heaven has been established and is now available for every man and woman. The Father has been glorified through the Son, and the destiny of all people can be altered to the reconciliation necessary for salvation to happen.

Before Jesus called out to the disciples to put the net on the right-hand side of the boat, He was doing something else. He brought some things with him to the sea like you or I would do. He had coals laid on a fire and fish cooking on a grill. The bread was warming on the edge of the grill. Verse nine says He had a charcoal fire already laid with fish and bread on it. After the disciples managed to get the large catch of fish to the shore, Jesus said to them "Come and have breakfast." They all knew at this time it was the Lord Jesus. Only Peter and John thought it could be the Lord before He invited them to eat the breakfast He was cooking for them. They knew because of the intimacy He was showing them by making breakfast and serving them.

The supernatural catch was not enough for all of them to recognize it was Jesus. Jesus says to them, bring Me some of the fish you have now caught. The first batch was ready to eat, and it was not part of the catch they made. The glorified Lord is now going to start the second batch, while the hungry boys do not have to wait more than a minute to start chowing down! I remember when I was young, and I would just make it home in time for dinner. It was always ready to eat when I was famished from playing baseball all day or basketball in the wintertime. My mother was such a blessing and a great cook. She was so concerned with making us a great dinner and feeding her family well. She was a good servant. At this point in the text, Jesus is only concerned with serving. The disciples sit down to eat while Jesus is preparing the second batch. He did not ask them to have breakfast with Him. He said come and have breakfast. He is not sitting with them until later, after all the food is done. He who came to serve and give his life for them has now become the Glorified Servant. You would think they would be kissing his glorified feet and bowing down in awe to Him. But, He is busy being the Host, the Baker, the Grill man, and the Waiter! He is serving them like a one-man restaurant service. He is doing it the same way we would have to do it.

Why did Jesus do it like we would have to do it? Could He not have spoken and have the food appear like He did when he fed the five thousand? The answer is this; Our God is humble, holy, and loving. He will always be very intimate with us. He told the disciples the greatest among you will be a servant to all. He is the greatest servant forever! With God, there is always intimacy with power and power with intimacy. There is a feeding and a resurrection or a resurrection and a feeding. He meets us in our frail human flesh and wants the depth of His love to change our lives. He condescends from being the supernatural, metaphysical King of the universe so He can meet us in intimate fellowship. Romans 6:18- tells us now that we are free from sin, we became servants of righteousness. It is a past tense fact of who we are in Jesus Christ.

Our master has shown us the way by His example. Humble and holy with love and service to all is the goal for God's children. Christ must be formed in us. Suppose you, as a man, could only do supernatural things with your wife. She would ask you to fix something, and you would say be fixed! And it would immediately happen all the time. Do you think your wife would be happy with you? You took the labor of love out of the situation as an equal correspondent. Where is the intimacy of loving service? It would be intimidating to her and make her feel inferior to you. There would not be an equal correspondence.

If one's wife could only do supernatural things for her husband, knowing how most men are, they would be out of the house very quickly. Jesus knows there is no love without humble service. For love to be valid, there must be a choice to serve another with the labor of love and keep an equal balance of power in the relationship. The little acts of kindness mean God is always at work. They are seeds of intimacy as we choose the labor of love as God commands us to do.

If Jesus did these things after His resurrection like He did before He rose, should we find it difficult to act out of who we are in Him? Should we not be serving each other out of love and with joy? In Luke 8:49-55, Jesus goes to see a twelve-year-old girl who has died. He tells them the girl is only sleeping, and they laugh at him. He enters the room, prays, and commands life back into her. She is raised from the dead! Does Jesus rebuke the people who laughed at him? No! He tells them to give her something to eat. There is a resurrection and a feeding that has taken place.

There is power with intimacy or intimacy with power. It is always this way with God. There's love with every miracle, and no miracles without love where God is concerned. If Jesus was like most men, He would have bragged and said; did you see what I did? Do you want to laugh at Me now? God does not want to intimidate people. He does not want to show off. He is humble and gentle in heart. In Matthew 11:29, Jesus says, Learn from Me, I am humble and gentle in heart, and you will find rest for your souls. He could have said learn from Me, I am almighty, omniscient, and omnipresent. All wisdom is in Me, I am the creator of life. I am self-existent. I am the miracle worker of love and healing. I am the eternal God. I am the Holy One! But, He said He was humble and gentle in heart because that is what all people need the most. Humility puts us in the correct place before our God to obey, love, and serve others. Gentleness will draw people to us and make them comfortable. When we are in submission to God, as servants of love, it brings relational success.

We share the gospel in word and deeds. The word of the Spirit is all powerful. The deeds of intimacy are God's love in action. This is the way of God and to become mature and holy in the Lord. It is a life yielded to our Lord, who has redeemed us from darkness and transferred us to His kingdom of light, love, and eternal life. See Ephesians 4:6 and Philippians 2: 12-13, which gives us a very interesting parallel in scripture. There is one God and Father who is:

1. Over all
2. Through all
3. In all

The order is submitting under His authority first, and then He works through us. After He works through us in a regular way, people will see God in us! The parallel verse says:

1. When we choose to obey, it shows God is over us.
2. God will help us work out our salvation through His good works.
3. It is His pleasure to choose and act in us by our humble submission to Him.

It will be Christ in us, the hope of glory. Let's look at Luke 12:37 NASB. Blessed are the servants who the master will find on the alert when He comes back; Truly, I say to you that He will gird himself to serve and have His servants recline at the table, and He will come to them and wait on them.

This sounds like the Host, the Baker, the Grill man, and the Waiter again! The greatest among you will be the servant to all. Jesus is the greatest servant in the universe! From the Suffering servant to Glorified servant forever. In heaven, Jesus will sit us down at the marriage supper of the Lamb. The obedient angels of God who have been His servants since they were created and always stayed under His authority will serve the saints the heavenly meal. Jesus will have half of a smile on His Glorified face, which is the smile of approval. He will say well done, good and faithful servants. We shall be together now and for all eternity. Amen!

Two flies on a clear clean window---
A Turn around Event!

There were two flies on a window that a cleaning service had just washed. It was in my business office when I was doing my paperwork. The two flies bounced up and down, trying to get out through the clean closed window. The sun was moving in and out of the clouds outside the window. The flies are always deceived by whatever instincts they have that a closed window is their way to freedom. You always see them on the windows. They are very persistent in their effort to get out, even though the glass will never permit it. They can even be said to be stubborn and stupid for the futile effort they are attempting.

I watched them and observed them for several minutes. I believe God wanted me to observe them. They started to get tired from bouncing and climbing up and down. Then I saw one of them fall dead at the base of the window. We have often found dead flies on the windowsills. This fly was deceived to the point of death. I was thinking about how he could have turned around, gone through the open door, and made his way back to the outside world. The second fly kept trying to get out through the clean window, and suddenly he turned 180 degrees and flew out of my open office door to get back outside. God was talking to me, and I started to write about it. Why did one of the flies refuse to turn around, and the other one make a 180 from the window to the freedom of the outside world where they both came from, to begin with? When the sun shines on a clear, clean window, you always see the areas of the window that still show deep ingrained dirt. Just like when you go to a carwash, and then the sun hits your window and exposes all the deep ingrained spots that only show up when the sun hits it.

Perhaps one of the flies could see the exposed dirt when the sun came out of the clouds and hit my office window. Maybe he realized his way was not as clean and clear as he thought it was. He may have known he was being deceived, trying to go the impossible way to freedom. But if he could recognize there was some deep dirt, what about the other fly who also saw the sun hit the window and refused to turn around and dropped dead, insisting it was the only way to go? We know flies carry bacteria and eat a lot of nasty things. They carry parasites. A parasite depends on other things to exist and does not give a return of life to any other organism. Selfish people can be like parasites on occasion, and everyone has some selfish things about themselves. It is in our sin nature, and we can say we need freedom from the selfish ways we behave. Like the flies that can bug us, people often tell another person to stop bugging them. Back to the fly who dropped dead. He did not respond the way the second one did and get to freedom.

Let's suppose the second fly had a way of recognizing the deeply ingrained dirt and knew his way was not perfectly clean and clear. Something may have prompted him to turn around and seek another way of escape. Suppose the first fly who died had the same awareness to prompt him but refused to turn around. When the sun shined on the window, he may have known his way was not as clean and clear by the ingrained spots of dirt, but he insisted on going one way only. He liked his own way in spite of the fact that it was dirty. Maybe he was blinded from banging his protruding eyeballs against the window too many times, trying to bounce his way through the window. Watching his effort, it was easy to see and say how stubborn and stupid the little creature was. He was not concerned with the dirt on his pathway, or he was blind to the truth that some dirt really existed. This is a clear reminder of the actions of many human beings. They are determined to go their way even if it will hurt them. They do not care how dirty their way may be, often pointing out someone else has more dirt to deal with than they do. Many people are blinded to their own faults or will not admit them because of pride, and they are acting as stubborn as the fly that refused to turn around. Whoever has heard the songs, (My Way) or (I Got to be me) could listen closely to the lyrics and see how deceived man is.

The scripture refers to it two times in the Proverbs and one time in the book of Jeremiah. Proverbs 14:12 and Jeremiah 10:23 confirm that man's way is the wrong way! There are two things that lead to death. Ignorance and willful rebellion. A person is just as dead by walking over the edge of a cliff, not knowing where the edge is as he would be if he chose to jump off. I walked outside my office and looked at all the windows in the shop where I worked. I saw a big bee lying dead at the base of one of the windows. I said, bee, where is your sting? The sting of death has also got you! Why did you not turn around? I walked back into my office to finish some paperwork and glanced at the window where the two flies started this message. Another fly came into the office and went right to the window. He started climbing and bouncing to get out, and after 30 to 40 seconds, he turned around and went back through the door to freedom. It came to my mind this could be the same fly that was in the office before and avoided death because he turned around, making a 180, through the door. If it was the same fly, he found himself back sliding on the window again.

Is there something we can relate to here? The fly was back, sliding on the window again. The fly could have remembered he was deceived before, and after trying his old way again, he said no more of this! Freedom comes through the door. Proverbs 14:12 speaks of the prideful way of man. Jeremiah 10:23-NASB says: I know, O Lord, that a man's way is not in himself. Nor is it in a man who walks to direct his steps. John 8:12 says, Jesus is the light of the world, and whoever follows Him will not walk in darkness but will have the light of life. Ephesians 5:13 says all things become visible when they are exposed by the light, for everything that becomes visible is light. Jesus Christ will shine His light on every human soul and expose all the sin of deep ingrained evil and wrongdoing that every man or woman has done from deep in their heart. They will not pass inspection, for there will be some dirt. One spot, and you will fall short of the glory of Our Holy God. Every person is responsible to come to the light. Jesus Christ is the light. He died in every person's place for their sins and offered them the way to the salvation of God.

John 3:20 says, some men love the darkness rather than the light, for their deeds are evil, and they will not come to the light for fear that they will be exposed. In John 10:9 NASB. Jesus says I am the door; if anyone enters through Me, he shall be saved and shall go in and out and find pasture. He says He is eternal life for all who believe in Him and trust in what He did on the cross for them. It takes a turnaround event that equals the word repent! Turnaround from your own way that leads to death and go through the door of salvation. I am calling all who will humble themselves and hear this truth to come forward to receive God's love and forgiveness. To the proud, I say you can go the way of the fly who refused to turn around. The choice is yours. The result will be the same! Or you can turn around and come through Jesus, who has the door to heaven open and His loving arms wide open to you, also. Lord, we thank you for being the door to Eternal life! Amen!

A Christmas Message for the present time!

I have a short multiple choice quiz consisting of five questions I am going to ask and I am looking for the correct answer. The questions will be listed from A to E. All the answers have some good points but only one answer is correct for the extremely important result that pertains to the question. The question is: What do people have to do to be raised from the first death and receive eternal life with God in the Kingdom of Heaven? Five choices to choose from please listen closely.

A. Be a good person and choose right from wrong. Let your conscience be your guide.

B. Knowing you are not perfect, make sure you don't do any real bad things like murder or rape which is what the big sinners do.

C. Make sure your good deeds far outweigh the wrong things you have done; showing God your profit and loss statement on how your assets are well above your liabilities in your behavior patterns.

D. Focus on helping others whenever you can; not thinking only about your own desires. Be other centered an unselfish. Find joy in giving yourself to others by serving them. Engage in good deeds.

E. Trust in what Jesus did on the cross as a substitute for our punishment because all people have sinned and fall short of God's perfect moral Holiness.

Knowing we do not compare ourselves with bigger sinners who act more wickedly than we do, but to a perfect Holy God who can't sin and died in our place. We must accept the fact that we can't measure up to God's standards by our own good deeds and our own inflated opinion of ourselves. We must bow down in humility and turn from our sins, from the small ones to the large ones. We confess we need God to save us and give us the gift of eternal life. A gift is not something we earn or deserve. We place our trust in Christ, alone, to save us and raise us to life after death to be reconciled to God forever. We must be humble to receive God's gift of eternal life. Pride will not receive it or say yes to God's incredible appeal through Jesus Christ. We exchange our sin for His righteousness, and we can live forever in a perfect, glorious, resurrected body. It is by His mercy and grace we are saved, not by any good things we have done.

What is the correct answer? A, B, C, D, or E? E is the correct answer. The answer to (E) is always first to enter heaven. This can lead us to do the things that are in the D answer. The grace and power of the Holy Spirit must come first, and He is the one who enables us to obey the serving life listed in the answer D. God gets the glory for any good work we do. We act by His Spirit in us, humble vessels for His purposes.

The Christian life starts with the E answer only. And speaking of the E answer, I remind you of what I said earlier in a previous chapter. God sent Jesus with His Eternal email 2000 + years ago. Jesus is the reason for Christmas, not Santa Claus or frosty the snowman. It is not the material stuff or the toys or the wonderful food or even the family get-together that makes for a Merry Christmas. The Savior entered the world to bring people the truth and to show people who God is and what He is like; Our Immanuel, God with us. God's loving gift came so He can reconcile the world back to Himself. We can come back into a proper relationship with a regenerated heart and mind. Our souls return to Him! This is the true reason for Christmas, and we all need to download the gospel message from our minds to our hearts and make sure it goes to saved mail. The facts are that God was in Christ reconciling the world to Himself, not counting our sins against us. The fullness of God's love comes with the reconciliation of each person choosing Him on an individual basis. Red, Brown, Yellow, Black, and White, everyone can get a metaphysical mega bite of the food that does not perish. Just open up God's Christmas Email and download it to the saved file of your heart. The Bible's text messages of love will tell us how to live God's way. It is amazing grace and indescribable love. Jesus said we should learn from Him in Matthew 11:28-29. Because He is humble and gentle in heart, we can find rest, freedom, and eternal life in Him alone! John 14:6 - Jesus is the way, the truth, and the life, and no one comes to our Father in heaven apart from Him. A warning I must give you; it takes humility! Drop all your pride and choose to bow to Jesus. He will exalt you to heaven and eternal life with God. I will end this Christmas message with a short poem:

Reconciliation Personified! --- Lord, take us back to where we belong with Christ in us, His presence strong! A child of creation has not the right stuff, but a child of redemption in Him is enough! As a matter of fact, God wants to own us twice! Since we have double with trouble, He paid double the Price!

Humility first for God to meet thirst!

God never boasts like a man will boast. Man has only one place where he should boast, and it is in the Lord only. (1 Corinthians 1:31). I counted over 70 questions God asks in the book of Isiah to reveal to us who He is and what He has done. When we can't come up with the answers, it reveals God's greatness. He does not want to intimidate us, and He is always humble and gentle in His communication with the people He loves. I counted over 60 questions in the book of Job where God brings Job to see he needs to repent for moving out from under the authority of God. Job was demanding answers because he was suffering so much. We can ask about our suffering, pray for God to remove it, or comfort us, but we can't get to the point where we are demanding answers and contending with God. Ref. Job 40:1. There is no wisdom and no understanding and no counsel against the Lord. (Proverbs 21:30). God gave Job a double blessing when it was all over, and His love is enough in any amount of suffering. Jesus suffered and conquered the grave in humility. All suffering has its seed in the pride against God. Humility brings victory to all who are in Christ. In Psalm 113:5-6 NASB, we see God's humility as creator and sovereign ruler. Who is like the Lord our God? Who is enthroned on high, who humbles Himself to behold the things that are in heaven and in earth? The truth is that humility is a permanent part of God's character. He loves everything He has made, and He always looks upon it with love and humility—ref Philippians 2:1-11.

We see the distinguishing feature of Jesus is humility. All the qualities of unselfishness are found in this passage of scripture. There is love, fellowship, affection, and being like-minded in unity of the Spirit. There is recognition of our proper and rightful place before God. There is never a place to strive for equality with God, and there is always a healthy fear of who He is. Ezekiel 28:17 is written to a man or group, and it easily takes us to the author of poison pride; Satan himself. It relates indirectly to Satan's fall. There is a very good description that indirectly relates to Satan's fall in Isiah 14:13-15. The Holy Spirit indirectly describes Satan's rebellion and pride and how he was cast out of heaven. It shows us how Satan corrupted himself. He refused to stay under God's authority. God has established His throne in the heavens, and His sovereignty rules over all. (Psalm 103:19) In Genesis 3:5, Satan decides to tempt Eve and tells her she can know as God knows. This is an impossible desire for the source of all knowledge did not create Himself. Everything He creates is something less than Himself, for He is the beginning of all creation and all of life. No created beings can be equal to who created them. There is a natural quest for knowledge in all people because we will always wonder about the amazing God who made us. Worship Him and live forever in honor, gratitude, and humility, knowing our rightful place before our amazing creator. Webster gives us a good definition of humility. The quality or state of being humble. Not proud or haughty, not arrogant, not comparing ourselves to others, expressing a spirit of deference or submission. This Spirit of submission is the key to life at its fullest level. God has three traffic signs for all of His children: This defines the Christian life> Warning Sign! Stop Sign! Yield Sign! God exalts the humble, and He causes the prideful to fall. Pride leads to destruction.

1 John 2:15-17 tells us that the lust of the flesh and the boastful pride of life is not from the Father (God) but from the world. God hates pride. Hear the humble approach of God when He addresses His people's sins in Isiah 48:18 NASB. If only you had paid attention to My commandments! Then your well-being would have been like a river, and your righteousness like the waves of the sea. Obeying God brings peace, power, and refreshment to ourselves and others. God has inspired His writers to pen many words so we can see the greatness of God without God boasting about Himself. All boasting of self is very insecure. There is no room for pride anywhere. It is not possible for God. He is eternally existent in the three persons of the Trinity. One in His essence and attributes yet completely other centered.

This is the amazing awesome God we have. If God says ME, referring to Himself, it is always US in the Godhead. If God says MY, referring to Himself, it always lines up with His –WE in the Godhead. He teaches Christian brothers and sisters the way it should be. Me, myself and I are never absent from we and us! We are to be other centered with unity and diversity as God's children. Each person is responsible and dependent at the same time. Complete independence is for God Himself in the Trinity. The Trinity maintains the power of Holiness, and the humility of God is necessary and in function at all times. God's humility is synchronized with His Holiness. It is a constant function of both. The personhood of God can never be separated as one person going a different way than the others. There is complete agreement in all situations. Isiah 43:13 God says, He is from eternity, and there is none who can deliver out of His hand. He says—if I act, who can reverse it? The question mark takes away the possibility of any insecure boasting. God is declaring what the truth is because there is no one greater than Him. It is a truthful declaration and not an insecure boast. Jesus referred to the Father as greater than Himself, so men who saw Him as a man would know He was sent from heaven to make the Father known. It is always the Father, the Son, and the Holy Spirit doing the work of the Trinity on all occasions. Jesus demonstrated the humility necessary for all men and women and the only way to glory. Being a true man and fully God, Jesus did not want men or women worshipping other men or women and exalting any human being above another person. The order of function and authority is shown in our amazing mediator to bring us to God! Jesus is now sitting at the right hand of the Father in the unapproachable light in the third heaven, as the Apostle Paul might have been describing in 2 Corinthians 12. Ref.) Jesus will come back as the Glorified Servant and the King of Kings. If we see Him, we see the Father and the Spirit that bonds all of life and love together. There is a healthy pride that is much different than destructive pride. This is why we can say that we are proud of some of the things we see people do or accomplish. It comes from love and approval. It comes from gratitude and having a healthy level of confidence in the things God has enabled us to do. The gratitude expressed is clothed in humility because, deep down, we don't take all the credit for what we are proud of. Everyone should realize the good accomplishments of men and women made in the image of God are always a gift from God. There should be a transfer of who gets the glory without men or women thinking they did it on their own. Listen to this powerful verse in Isiah 44:8b NASB. Is there any God besides Me, or is there any other Rock? I know of none." The rock is indicating the only foundation to build on. God is the reason, love, and power behind all people who do good things, whether they give Him the glory or not. It is the common grace of being made in the image of God. No one lives without the breath of God every minute they breathe. God knows of no other place to discover or build your life upon than to build it upon Him. We must realize we were made for His glory and only live for Him. It is a waste of time and life to worship idols or put anything ahead of God. Ref. Isiah 57:15 speaks so clearly of a man's call to be humble before God and how God can exalt people to a higher level of living under His love and authority. Our Holy, Humble God wants to condescend and meet us at our own level and bring us to a higher level of living in Him. We must realize our dependence upon Him and how much we need to be under His authority. This results in perfect love and security. God makes His home with the humble and contrite of heart. Just to mention a few questions God directly asks Job, we will see God's greatness by His humble approach. Can you control the movement of the stars? Can you ensure the sequence of the seasons? Can you shout to the clouds and make it rain? Have you ever commanded the morning to appear and caused the dawn to appear in the east? Job 40:1 NLT is the best question to bring repentance. Do you still want to argue with the Almighty? You are God's critic, but do you have the answers? The next question from God proves there is only one remedy for man's poison of pride. It's in Job 40:12. Can you look on everyone who is proud and humble them, and tread down the wicked where they stand? This is like asking Job if he is the righteous judge against all the destructive pride on the whole earth. The One and only judge of the universe is engaged in a conversation with one man. How privileged is it for a man to receive this great correction that is taking place? The final question I will mention; God asks in Job 41:11: who has given to Me that I should repay him? Whatever is under the whole heaven is Mine. It is a rhetorical question leaving no answer or the one obvious answer-No one! We are obligated to be humble before God and love and obey His Word. The next question is for all Christians to receive as an absolute instruction for well-being. Micah 6:8- What does the Lord require from us? (Answer) To do justice, to love kindness and mercy, and to walk humbly with your God. Doing what's right, showing God's love to all, and walking as an empty vessel with the humility of Jesus Christ living His life through us. Humility can't be separated from God's love.

In 1 Corinthians 13: 4-8 NIV, Love is patient, love is kind, it does not envy, It does not boast, it is not proud, it is not rude, it is not self-seeking. These qualities of love are the same qualities of humility. A prideful person can't love God's way. The motive would be self-glory, and pride does not give the glory to God. God is love in the truest sense of the word. Love is humble. Pride is self-centered, and love is always other centered. A humble person does not speak of the good deeds they do. They do not do them to impress others or pat themselves on the back for their actions. The humble person obeys and loves in submission to God's two great commandments. Loving God first and foremost and loving others as we love ourselves. Humility always has a teachable spirit. Jesus tells His followers to learn from Him, and they do what He says. God's blessing and relief in times of trouble will always come from submission to Him. We surrender for His splendor. 1 Peter 5:6 says- Humble yourselves under the mighty hand of God, and He will exalt you at the proper time. James 4:7 Submit therefore to God resist the devil, and he will flee.

Keep this acronym. Submission:

Staying Under By Much Intended Spiritual Strength In Our Nature

The intended strength always being the Holy Spirit. It is part of the nature of Jesus, and it must be formed in us. To be made holy can only come to the humble people of God. The proud who claim righteousness will never attain true righteousness. The self-righteous man will die apart from God if he does not humble himself. We are greatly privileged to have a humble and holy God who can get past the flesh nature in us and impart His humble love to us. We must stay humble.

When Jesus gave the disciples the power over the demons in Luke 9:51-56, He had to remind them not to rejoice in that power but to be glad their names were written in heaven. If you ever try to go against evil forces by the pride of the flesh and without calling on Jesus, you will experience a huge defeat, and evil will beat you up inside. Only Jesus can beat the evil out of you! God would like to beat the evil out of everyone! He came to remove it! Ref. 1 John 3:5 and John 1:29. We must guard against pride and realize God gets the glory all the time. When God works through us, we can learn to say: Lord, it is a privilege and a pleasure to watch you work! We never call for fire to come down on our enemies when we are humble. We give everything to God. He is the pilot light that fuels the fire in our Spirit. We run on His G.A.S. God's Available Spirit. He is the driver at the wheel as we travel along. He is the Captain of the ship, and we are His first mates. He is the King of Kings, and we are His faithful subjects. We are vassals with victory over hassles in submission to our King. We are His children holding His hand, listening closely to His commands.

When we are shocked or alarmed, we are carried in His arms! There is a song to sing that will please our king! It's called- All of me, Lord, take all of me! Submission to God means submission to other people most of the time. But there will be times when we should not submit to people when it involves disobedience to God. When the gospel was given at Pentecost, the Holy Spirit came in power, and all the Apostles and disciples began a journey to become humble. You can see clearly that beyond their spiritual functional gifts given by God, they knew being a servant to all was of the utmost importance. They focused on their function for Christ, and as they grew in sanctification, they realized who they became in Christ, Bond Servants of God. How many Christians are living out their new life and dying to the old life which was crucified with Christ? (Galatians 2:20.) Jesus was the greatest servant of all. He was the suffering servant, and he became the glorified servant after the resurrection. Completely absent from self-centeredness in the power of the Trinity, we have a humble awesome God, and all people will be humbled under Him. Every knee will bow to the King of Kings. (Philippians 2:10.) When Jesus comes back, He will serve the servants who served Him doing His will. What a privilege for all who are His servants. We must be humble and grateful and obey our Lord and Savior. What do we have that has not been given to us? Ref. 1 Corinthians 4:7. Let him who boasts boast only in the Lord! (1 Corinthians 1:30) Do we know the Grace of the Lord Jesus Christ? Do we know that for our sake, He became poor and that we can become rich through His poverty? The everlasting glory of eternal riches and eternal life is ours when we are conformed to the likeness of the King of Kings. Glory is for certain, and we will rejoice with exaltation when He brings us home. We are all equally loved by God, and we are equally responsible to come to Him to be saved. There is room at the cross for you! Don't miss the call of God. It is why we exist. It is amazing that we have such a glorious opportunity. Bow down to Jesus and be lifted from your sins, humility must be first, and God will always meet thirst. Say yes to the Lordship of Jesus Christ.

Gentleness is the Glove of Love for the Humble Hand!

Nothing is better than being wise and knowing how to interpret the meaning of life. Wisdom puts light in the eyes and gives gentleness to words and manners. Eccl. 8:1. The Message Bible. There are two main signs in this verse for being wise. God's anointing shows on the face and in the eyes of a person, and the character of Christ is always gentle. Humility is the heart and hand of love, and gentleness is the glove of love for the humble hand. James 3:13 NASB--Who among you is wise and understanding? Let him show by his good behavior his deeds in the gentleness of wisdom. This is a parallel verse to confirm the importance of gentleness. Where there is wisdom, there is gentleness. They are not separated. Are we demonstrating wisdom by a gentle spirit? In Matthew 11:29, Jesus tells us gentleness with humility is the way to find rest in our souls. We know there are many things we can learn about Jesus, but He shows a strong focus on gentleness and humility because that is what we may need the most to be close to God and others. It demonstrates love and godliness. James 3:17 describes wisdom from above, and it includes gentleness and confirms wisdom is always gentle. Gentleness is a fruit of wisdom, and it is in the fruit of the Spirit in Galatians 5:22-23. The opposite of gentleness would be harsh or overbearing. It is hard to like a person who lacks gentleness. You can love past harshness, but it is not likable. God's Word speaks to husbands on how they should love their wives. Colossians 3:19 NLT. You husbands must love your wives and never treat them harshly. God is saying it, and it is important to obey it. Being gentle is something that can be learned, for we who are in Christ have the Holy Spirit and His fruit within us. Ask for it and yield to Him.

The opposite of harshness is gentleness. Ask your wife, sweetheart, am I being gentle with you? Take an inventory and get her honest opinion. Let us look at a verse of scripture that may surprise many of the men who read it—Psalm 18:35 NASB. You, God, have given me the shield of your salvation, and your right hand upholds me, and your gentleness makes me great. David writing the words of the Spirit and declaring God's gentleness makes him great. How many people would associate gentleness with greatness? It is extremely important in our character and will draw people to Jesus, the Lamb of God. Most women would describe a nice guy by the kindness and gentleness he shows. It is a positive and not a negative where love is concerned. If he is cool and calm, he may be a gentle person, and the same thing applies to women with their husbands.

Prov. 15:1 says: A gentle answer turns away wrath, but a harsh word stirs up anger. This is the way all of us need to communicate.

Proverbs 25:15 says through patience, a ruler can be persuaded, and a gentle tongue can break a bone. (Gentle speech can crush opposition) A bone is hard and stiff, and stiff opposition can be broken down by gentleness. It can penetrate the hardness of a person's heart! It can be a softener to the soul. Jesus came riding in on a donkey very gently, bringing righteousness a week before He was crucified. God's approach is not concerned with a grand entrance like the celebrities in the world would make. Gentleness makes a slow entrance into people's lives. And once it does, it causes people to stick around. The slow entrance into people's lives is like moving toward the beach ball in the water. If you move too fast, the ball will get further away from you. You are compelled to slow down to get closer to the desired object. Gentleness is completely compatible with patience. How is your approach? Are you moving into people's lives like the gentle Lamb of God with an attitude and disposition of gentleness? The gentle, patient approach has positive results.

1. You don't make waves!
2. You are not perceived like a Piranha fish!
3. You do not disturb or disrupt by force!
4. You do not evoke fear by being too loud or noisy!
5. You will not be like a pit bull but completely tamed and under control.
6. There will not be any barking!
7. There will be no lion roaring!
8. You will draw people to the character of Jesus Christ! If you are doing effective witnessing gentleness is the way to draw people to God.

Your goal is to let the Holy Spirit create the currents that guide them to see Jesus in you. Only He can draw them to salvation. Your gentleness can draw people to see your effective witness. Jesus told the disciples in John 12:32 that if I am lifted up from the earth, I will draw all men to myself. People are thirsty for the truth and the love of God in their soul. We try to meet their thirst a little bit at a time. The Apostle Paul asked the disobedient Christians in 1 Corinthians 4:21 NASB. What do you desire? Shall I come to you with a rod or with love and a spirit of gentleness"?

I interpret this as saying it would be better to learn the easy way than the hard way of tough love. The Holy Spirit wants to impart His gentleness any time we need correction. It is so tender and more accepting to receive correction by our gentle God than to get some real tough consequences. Our cooperation and submission to God would help us avoid some of the tougher forms of discipline. God will work His way into our sanctification process, doing whatever is necessary, but our responses do make a difference. It is a process we must adhere to. Gentleness is like glue. People will stick around when you are gentle. Love that is bonding is love that will stay with us, and very few people would run from a gentle person. Gentleness helps us stick together without feeling stuck. There is freedom in a spirit of gentleness. Listen how the church is being encouraged by Paul.

In Ephesians 4:1-2b, Paul tells the church to walk in a manner worthy of the calling they received with all humility and gentleness, and patience. Humility and gentleness get things started with no walls going up. It breaks down defensive patterns so love can be established. It is the best approach when it's a spirit of humility and gentleness. Being gentle is a preservative. It keeps things from being spoiled or damaged, or even destroyed. A woman may buy a new set of China wanting some valuable dishes. Two things she might say when someone handles them. Be careful with those dishes. Don't drop them. Or she might say be gentle handling those dishes. I don't want them to break or get damaged. Gentle can be synonymous with careful. Careful can be taken as full of care. Treat them like they are precious. Gentleness is an important fruit of the Holy Spirit. Gentleness is the quality of handling something with care. The next verse that needs to be shared is specifically for the men.

1 Thessalonians 2:7 NASB, speaking about three powerful men of God, Paul, Timothy, and Silas--- "But we proved to be gentle among you, as a nursing mother tenderly cares for her own children." Comparing the three men with a nursing mother should tell all men that love requires gentleness and just how important it is. Some men may have trouble accepting this verse, but after Paul, Timothy and Silas learned from God, they knew the fruit of gentleness. Ladies and Gentlemen! Does this announcement include you? Men of God take heed of this. It is the way of Jesus.

In 1 Peter 3:1-4- We are told that the inner beauty of a wife is more important than the outer beauty. It tells us that a gentle spirit can help an unbelieving husband come to salvation. Gentleness is an unfading beauty in a woman. Character is forever! Isiah 40:11 speaks of a male shepherd who gently leads the female sheep who are nursing their newborn sheep. A caring husband and father who is gentle with his family will form a bond of love with them.

Galatians 6:1- speaks of correction to a person caught in sinful behavior. It must be done in a spirit of gentleness, so the one doing the correcting is not tempted himself. There must not be a judgmental spirit. Having a gentle approach when helping one who struggles with sin demands our sensitivity and gentleness. Prayer must come first because we need God and His gentleness to minister through us. When facing opposition, we correct only in a spirit of gentleness. It is a careful approach, so the walls of self-protected patterns are not erected. The walls must come down, and new life and love can enter. If needed, take a few days or weeks until you know the time is right. Gentle love and peace have more than just a chance with God at work. When we empty ourselves and ask God to fill us with a gentle spirit, we find out what a pleasure it is to watch Him work! God wants to see all people potentially under the blood of Jesus. His gentle love is for all. I want to compare gentleness with boldness to show the power of gentleness. Paul speaks to the church with this approach.

2 Corinthians 10:1a (NIV) By the meekness and gentleness of Christ, I appeal to you.) Boldness is good at times, but it often has negative connotations. Gentleness has nothing negative in the definition. Boldness can mean courage and strength with a fearless spirit which is good. This is the only boldness quality we should show. It also means impudent, presumptuous, and contemptuous with a cocky disregard for others; insolent, harsh, and overbearing. Gentleness is a much better preference to have over boldness. Gentleness has nothing but good qualities. It is honorable, distinguished, kind, amiable, and free from harshness, sternness, or violence. Gentleness shows balance, and boldness can be out of balance unless it is tempered by gentleness. Jesus is the lion of Judah one time in Revelation from courage and the power of His victory only! He is the Lamb of God more than 20 times.

What is His preference? Boldness is not listed in the fruit of the Spirit in Galatians 5:22-23. Gentleness is mentioned. Bold is only to be taken as being courageous and without fear. If some people could see themselves like others see them when they are being bold, they might decide to keep their boldness to themselves. People who are being bold handle their own boldness a lot easier than others may be able to handle it! Do others receive your boldness, or do they have to survive it? REMEMBER THIS QUIP! I needed it for myself first, and that's why God gave it to me in my time of solitude. (God's Wrath has been appeased! Gentleness Please!)

We are never persuasive when we're abrasive! Colossians 3:12 tells us, as God's people, to clothe ourselves with compassion, kindness, humility, gentleness, and patience. Bold clothes are not mentioned. Boldness is needed occasionally, but make sure you limit it to fearless and courageous. Calm and pleasant attitudes are God's preference. 1 Timothy 6:11 tells us to flee from evil things and pursue righteousness, godliness, faith, love, perseverance, and gentleness. Are we beginning to see the importance of gentleness in our disposition?

1 Peter 3:15 NASB. But sanctify Christ as Lord in your hearts, always be ready to make a defense to everyone who asks us to give an account for the hope that is in you, yet with gentleness and reverence. It is very important in our witness for Christ. Gentleness will not be pushy or start an argument with those who are not yet in the faith as we are. Gentleness draws questions from others about our real faith. The truth can't help but be seen by others through the Spirit who indwells us, and He is always bearing His fruit of gentleness. The Holy Spirit is a smooth operator, and He can make our witness for Jesus an easy experience. We carry the most crucial reconciliation possible, which is available for all. If we are challenged with a question from others, we must respond with gentleness and reverence to every person made in the image of God. We raise Christ up, and we don't raise our voices. The walls come down as gentleness breaks the hardness. We are fearless with gentleness in character. Perfect love casts out all fear in others. Love is courageous, and God's gentleness in us shows His greatness. (Psalm 18:35)

A question for all of us; Are we as bold as the lion and as gentle as a lamb? There are two different lions in the bible. There is the lion of Judah, the one who is the King of Kings and who is more often referred to as the Lamb of God on the throne.

Ref. Revelation 5:5. There is also the roaring lion who seeks to devour people. 1 Peter 5:8 NASB Be of sober Spirit, be on the alert. Your adversary, the devil, prowls around like a roaring lion, seeking someone to devour. This lion is a thief that comes to steal, kill and destroy, but Jesus, the Lamb of God, came to bring abundant life, life to the fullest quality! Ref. John 10:10. Satan is absent from the fruit of the Holy Spirit. He is devoid of God's character, which includes gentleness. He may sometimes try to imitate God, but the roar is always waiting to come out. Gentleness and kindness from the Spirit can't be faked. It has to be real, for God is always humble, holy, and faithful. I believe many people need to realize the importance of body language and the tone of words. If it's the Holy Spirit's work in us, the fruit of the Spirit will be present. Ninety-Three percent of communication is body language and tone. Many brilliant counselors teach this. If the body language is warm and open and the tone is kind and gentle, the content will be believed and received as the honest truth. It is true people lie and deceive others by their words, but we can get discernment from God, who will help us when we submit to His authority and love. He reveals the truth, and we are always grateful. You can learn to read body language, and it's easy to recognize when a tone is harsh and abrasive. Pride can be recognized in body language and certainly in the boastful tone that comes out. We are all in the process of being tempered and refined by the Refiner's fire. The God who transforms us into the image of our Lord and Savior, Jesus Christ. What a privilege to know God through Christ!

We can be forever grateful. Let's look at Revelation 5:5 and try to absorb it into our spirits. John is writing from the vision God is giving him. He says, one of the elders said to me, stop weeping; behold the lion from the tribe of Judah, the root of David, Jesus has overcome so as to open the book and its seven seals. NASB. This is the only time the lion is described as Jesus because He won the victory and conquered the grave for all of us. But then John sees the seven Spirits of God and the Lamb who was slain for us. The only way to get the throne was for Him to be the Lamb of God who obeyed the Father's will dying in our place. He redeemed all of mankind and brought salvation to all who trust Him. Jesus the Lamb takes the book of judgment from the right hand of the Father and the seven Spirits of God and prepares to open the seven seals for the end is coming. Jesus is worthy to be the king of the universe by His humility and gentleness and, of course, His holy perfect love by obeying the Father's will. John heard the elder say, stop weeping. All weeping is coming to an end!

Look at Revelation 7:17 (NASB). It is the Lamb who is in the center of the throne. (The lion is in submission to the Lamb) It is the Lamb who will be our shepherd and shall guide us to springs of the water of life and will wipe away every tear from our eyes. The elimination of sorrow as we know it. Joy everlasting with life eternal through Jesus Christ! Evil will be confined to the lake of fire, never to cause harm or malfunction of life again. Gentleness keeps the destructive pride away. Boldness can be vulnerable to destructive pride. One of the negative parts of boldness is being harsh and abrasive.

Harshness is like a bad thunderstorm where the wind blows, and the trees are ready to snap some branches off. The lightning and thunder is rolling, and we can read it as a frightful reminder there is disorder in the world. We know a bad storm can cause heavy rain and flooding. It can cause damage and sometimes loss of life. If it is a severe storm with the potential for tornados, it can be devastating to property and endangering people's lives. We can see a sense of judgment in a very bad storm as a reminder that nature was subjected to the fall of man after sin entered the world. We always want a bad storm to stop when it is out of control, and we are glad when it calms down. Gentleness is like a soft rain coming straight down without any high winds and no thunder or lightning. I can say I love a steady soft rain that comes straight down, knowing God is giving us the necessary water to bring growth to the crops and trees. He is causing fruit to be produced for all of us to enjoy. A steady rain coming straight down is speaking peace to the earth. The ground gets a soft penetration of water, and it absorbs the water without it rolling off by hitting it too hard. The lower ground does not collect all the water when it comes down slow and steady and covers all the ground evenly. There is a sweet smell after a soft, steady rain, and the gentleness of creation is manifested in a soft, steady rain. God is saying I love you through the steady falling rain, and all of you can enjoy yourselves by the water that provides the necessities for maintaining growth and life.

The bottom line is there is no destruction in a calm, soft rain. Ref. Matthew 5:45 tells us God sends His rain on the righteous and the unrighteous knowing how much He loves everyone! Gentleness is also like a refreshing drink of water. But it's only refreshing when you get a chance to breathe and swallow it correctly. Harshness is like trying to pour a drink down without taking a breath or the time to swallow it properly. It can choke the life out! If we, as the people of God, strike like lightning and come in like thunder, we will certainly drive people away or destroy our relationships. In the first Rocky movie, Rocky's trainer Mickey tells him he has to become a dangerous person. He tells Rocky he has to eat lightning and release thunder! A good description of the danger of being harsh and abrasive is lightning and thunder. But we don’t want to be dangerous to people we meet or know. We want to remove fear or melt down the walls of fear. When we love God's way, we come in like a soft, gentle rain into a person's life. We bring the living water of the Holy Spirit. We don't cause a flood of trouble and violent acts that can be destructive. We penetrate the hardness and soften the hearts of others with God's gentleness. I will close on this topic with five statements to remember the importance of gentleness in our character. God started showing me my need for gentleness with my pet bird, a female cockatiel. If I moved toward her too fast or quick or speaking too loudly, her feathers got ruffled, and she would fly to another place in the room. When I moved really slow and quietly, she would stare at me, fluff her feathers, and not move her feet from the perch. Then she would come right on my finger. I have five quips to share that I hope we can all remember.

1. You don’t have to ruffle a person’s feathers when you know how to fluff them!
2. If you start with a ruffle you will end up with a scuffle!

3. When you have the right stuff you will learn how to fluff! (Gentleness)
4. Harsh and rough will be too tough but soft and sweet just can't be beat!
5. God's wrath has been appeased! -→→-→ <u>GENTLENESS PLEASE!</u>

Prayer: Lord take the roaring lion away! The one who devours please keep him at bay! But the Lamb of God let Him live through me! Bringing Gentleness in Wisdom and setting people free!

Gentleness is like glue. It will cause people to stick with you!

Humility is synchronized with Holiness; in perfect Harmony always!

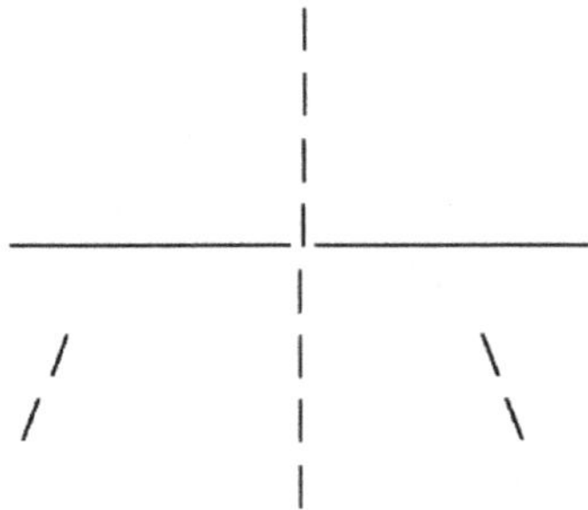

The heart and hand of Humility is first for God to meet everyone's thirst! True!

The glove of Gentleness fits perfect. It's learning what Jesus wants for us to live like Him! True!

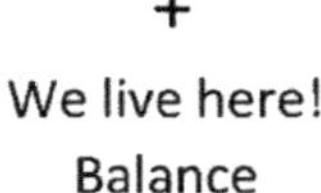

Learn from Me for I am humble and gentle in heart and you will find rest for your soul. My yoke is easy. My burden is light. (Jesus) Matthew 11:29-30 NIV

Gods Fellowship in Himself Where Perfect Love Starts!

One in His Essence and Three in His Personhood

God is the perfect communicator and the perfection of love that fills His universe. It is possible to imagine each person of the Trinity saying this, "I am One, and We are Three. I give to two others, and they give back to Me. Because this happens, We are complete and free. Love forever flows from the Trinity!" We are inclined to agree with this statement. God in three persons would relate perfectly without being self-centered! There is a two-to-one ratio of love and communication in God by Himself. One gives and two receive. One speaks, and two listen. This is the amazing personhood of the Trinity, always other-centered! As children of God, we can practice this two-to-one ratio differently. We could say," I am one, and we are three; there's God, my neighbor, and there's me. I can give to two others and keep some for me, and when this happens, love covers all three." I love my neighbor through the action of good deeds and kind words. I love God by obeying His command to love Him with all my whole heart, soul, and mind and to love my neighbor as myself. I love God separately when I am alone and resist the temptation to sin. This, of course, is the ideal situation. But, because of free will and the sin nature of all people, we can practice love, and our neighbor might not receive it. Our neighbors include our brothers and sisters in Christ. When we don't receive love back from our neighbors or brothers and sisters, we must remember that God always gives us a return. We still receive God's love from all three persons in His personhood. Here are some facts; when my neighbor, brother, or sister doesn't give back to me, I still receive from the presence of three. God, in three persons, has promised me His love will flow from the Trinity. (Romans 5:5).

The love of God has been poured into our hearts as believers in Jesus. He has given us the Holy Spirit in a full provision of love. When I obey the command to love, I will always get a supernatural return of love in my soul. When my neighbor, my brother, or my sister gives back to me, I am receiving from five persons' presence. Every act of real love can't be separated from God. For God in three persons plus my neighbor, a brother or sister is five. When this happens, I will surely thrive. It is okay to divide the personhood of God into three because He is three persons in one essence. We are not dividing the essence of God in any way, for He is ONE in His Essence and all three persons are equally God! It is possible to receive from more than five persons as long as you consider God as the three persons He is. There can be an abundance of love flowing through unhindered channels. Now, it's time to point out the reality of sin and those who choose to hate God and believe they are in complete control of their own life. Their pride and rejection lead them to the principle of unbelief. This is how their dilemma goes; they would say, I am one, and there's only me. I'll give to no one; keep it all for me. For me, myself and I are the one, and that is all I need to get life done! MALFUNCTION! MALFUNCTION!

No connections are bred! God's love has stopped flowing the guy's breathing, but he's dead! For the greatest commandment, the Father has said is clearly written, or have you not read Matthew 22:37-39? Love the Lord your God with your whole being; (Heart, Soul, and Mind,) and love your neighbor as yourself. Let's all say this together because we want to live a life of love. "I am one, and we are three; there's God, my neighbor, and there's me. I give to them, and they give back to me, and when this happens, we all start to see! There's life and love through the Trinity! And it flows from God through my neighbor and me!" We find this two-to-one ratio in God can be practiced by husbands and wives when they submit to be other-centered in love. The average woman speaks twice as much as the average man. Does this mean women talk too much or men don't listen well enough? God wants the man to be a leader in the home and to understand His wife. We have two ears and one mouth, and I think we all, men and women, can benefit from using the two-to-one ratio in our relationships.

We are made in God's image, and He gave us the two-to-one features in our makeup to help us relate like Him. God wired most women to know more about how a relationship should be. Perhaps it happened in the fall of Adam and Eve that God left the woman knowing more about how a relationship should be. We all need to be understood and listened to. Lord, help us all, husbands and wives, to be sensitive to each other and hear what is being said past all the words to what is in our hearts. The same Holy Spirit is in all of us, and He is the sensitivity of God and the one who conveys the help we all need to live in love with each other. This applies to all people to love the correct way. We listen well to show love to our children, friends, and everyone around us. From our neighbors to relatives and all the people we meet and come in contact with, we need to listen well. It can be effective with people across the world who we contact through the internet or cell phones. Love is the fullness of God and the goal of our instruction from start to finish!

1 Timothy 1:5 NASB is the start. The goal of our instruction is love from a pure heart, a good conscience, and sincere faith.

Ephesians 3:19 NASB is the finish line; to know the love of Christ which surpasses knowledge that you may be filled up to all the fullness of God. Consider God's two-to-one ratio in every relationship! Listen well and love well!

A Suitable Helper

Suitable:

Let's look at this word closely. We see two words together in this one word. Suit and able. A suit has to fit perfectly before a person can wear it. It often needs a taylor to alter it according to the person's body structure. God knows how to make alterations in people to help them relate in love His way. A suit has to fashion you to look better. The Bible tells us God fashioned Eve from one of Adam's ribs, which was how He made her. If you are one of a married couple, I have a question for you. A question for the husband first. Is your wife a good fit for you? Can she make you look better? A question for the wife; is your husband a good fit for you? Does he make you look better? Are both of you able to be stronger and much healthier together? Can both of you say: She suits me just fine or he suits me just fine! Is your marriage a real good fit? Or is there something causing a split? Are you helping each other do God's will? Or is there contention and strife making both of you ill? Is there submission, commitment, complete oneness no shame? Or pride and enmity, self-will and blame? How do you score it if your marriage needs more? If only you knew what God has in store! Submit to each other and find peace with God's rest! God's plan is to bless you and give you His best! You can both come to say my marriage suits me fine. We are able and blessed from God's love, and that's Divine!

A Suitable Helper is from God

Is Variety the Spice of Life?

We have often heard the statement that variety is the spice of life. Meaning: doing a lot of interesting things by choosing a wide assortment. To experience and experiment in many different areas and places and having different types and forms. A good word to describe it is being multifarious; a wide assortment to choose from. But, variety becomes impropriety when it involves sexual activity with more than one special mate. Sex is for marriage only. God has made this clear in His word. Having sexual variety is not the spice of life it's the lice of life. It will suck the life out of you and bring destruction upon you. Yes! Sexual attraction is a key ingredient inside all of us. It is part of our essence and nature designed to make up for wholeness in marriage.

The Bible note from the NIV Application Bible in 1 Corinthians 6:18 reads, God has created sex to be an essential and beautiful ingredient of marriage. It is A KEY INGREDIENT IN MARRIAGE! This means that no one who is married or single should open up a BAKERY! One favorite Cake or Cookie is proper in marriage. THUS SAYS THE LORD! For all of the men, I am telling you this; your wife is the only Cake you are to consume. And your wife is the only Cookie that should have all your looking >>> AFTER<<< the marriage has been hooking! (This can apply to the wives also). The woman it does apply to can read the message reversing the gender from men to women and from wife to husband.

How a man should love a woman God's Way!

1. Serve her as an equal correspondent with every day acts of kindness and generosity. He takes the initiative even if she does not. It's always his turn to initiate the kindness. He does not think like, I will do this for her is she does such and such for me first. This kind of thinking would go against God's law of sowing and reaping. It would not show unconditional love.
2. He listens to her with focused attention. He makes direct eye contact and has open arms. He hears more than words. He reads her body language and he hears her heart. He recognizes the painful areas and knows how to minister to them. He verifies her words. He validates her. He values her. He enjoys her because she is a gift from God to him. He encourages her and edifies her daily.
3. He gives her the labor of love in sharing the everyday chores and all the mundane things that this life presents.
4. He spends himself on her with all his energy and has a zeal to keep things fresh and exciting.
5. He protects her at all times. He is ready to die for her safety. He is stronger physically but they are one flesh. He loves himself and will protect himself so he does the same for her; even if he loses his life doing it. He prays the word of God over her life and believes God's angels will guard her with a hedge of power. Whenever she needs protection he is watching over her with God and angels and believes she will be safe for God is with both of them.
6. He gives her little notes of love when they are not together by leaving them on the table or the bathroom mirror.
7. He overlooks her imperfections and flaws because love covers a multitude of transgressions. He knows he has many imperfections and flaws and he wants to set an example of unconditional acceptance.
8. He does not keep score or point the finger at all. They win together by submission and cooperation!

9. When overlooking her mistakes or flaws there is no need to say anything some of the time. He is not the judge. But he is also overlooking the situation like a policeman on patrol. He is in charge to superintend the relationship if he sees something that needs to be discussed or needs attention. He confronts her in a spirit of gentleness. He is being a good fruit inspector and she is a good fruit inspector for him. They are to resolve confusion and conflict and work to build the intimacy that establishes reconciliation and forgiveness to the relationship on a constant basis. Love overlooks both of these ways and love always overcomes!

10. He consults his partner on all the important decisions they make. He respects her God given intuition and her strong sense on relational matters. If he does not do this the decision is a halfhearted one. The two of them are in oneness in the Spirit and the two hearts must agree on all important decisions. This makes it a wholehearted decision.

11. He practices gentleness and humility toward his partner. Why should he ruffle her feathers when God has given him the ability to fluff them? He does his good deeds in the gentleness of wisdom. Jesus said we should learn from Him for He is gentle and humble in heart. A man is a man when he has learned from Jesus. A man avoids strife and arguments with a gentle approach and he is a peacemaker. He sets the tone with gentleness and humility to resolve issues at a peaceful level.

12. He maintains a spirit of gratitude to God at all times. He knows God has given him the replacement of his missing rib. He now has the physical and emotional outlet for the best human relationship that can help complete him. He, also, has the spiritual blessing from God who is at work in her to bless him back. The best human relationship is enhanced by a spirit of gratitude. Give thanks to God who enables each partner to love the Lord's way. Give thanks with a grateful heart.

13. He always loves God first and it is his primary priority. He is God's first mate. God is the captain of his life. He does not compromise his love for God or put his wife ahead of God. (Adam made this mistake).This man worships the giver and not the wonderful gift God has given him in his partner. He who finds a good wife obtains favor from the Lord. Proverbs 18:22. NASB.

14. He enjoys his partner for who she is. The one God has given him exclusively! He does not put his focus on what she can give him. He plants love into her hoping for a return but never demanding it! If she is getting God's love from him she will

respond with a return by her voluntary choice to love him back. Love makes the universe go around and God's way is the only correct choice to make.

15. He loves his partner by his free will choice and this validates his love. He is not forced to love her or coerced in any way. But, there will be times when he does not want to love or feel like it. He must go to a higher level in love. He must go past his feelings and his flesh nature, his moods and his selfishness and his own will and do God's will! God says to husbands, love your wives as Christ loves the church. Jesus said to the Father, Not my will but your will be done. Jesus wanted out of the garden thinking of how his flesh nature would suffer but still obeyed the command of the Father to go to the cross. He loved out of obligation without feeling like it or wanting it in His flesh nature. When a man obeys the command to love even when he does not want to or feel like it he still produces the right action of love toward his mate. There is an obligation factor to choose the correct response to God out of gratitude for what God has done for all of us. We owe love to people because we could never repay God for His infinite love for us. Ref. Romans 13:8 says-Owe nothing to anyone except the continuing debt to love others. This is a debt you can never finish paying! We owe love payments to all people and especially to our most exclusive relationship, after the one with God, with our wife or husband. Obligation to obey in love supersedes our feelings and our flesh nature that hinders many of the correct choices to love. Love is the correct action with or without your feelings in agreement!

16. The man who loves his wife knows he has two mandates from God. The spiritual one and the cultural one. He has to demonstrate a strong work ethic and be willing to do whatever it takes to provide spiritual and material needs. When the spiritual is primary the emotional, material, and physical needs must function in a healthy way for it is all written in the word of God. The man is diligent and determined and steady and balanced in the two mandates. He is also very flexible at certain times like a branch that is filled with the vine. He will handle adversity and tough times when they come and bounce back from all of them. Back to trusting God for all the provision. He will bend for his wife or adapt and overcome by honoring God. He knows he works for God first and takes care of his loved ones by doing whatever is necessary. He believes the word and promises of God without wavering.

17. He knows three kinds of love for his partner; Unconditional, intimate friendship, and passionate sexual love. (Agape, Philia, and Eros) and this is really the best order to remember for the relationship to perform the vows of the covenant they made before God. This order helps it go the distance! God hates divorce. More divorce takes place when people do not love unconditionally and when they do not have a solid springboard of friendship for the foundation to deeper love.

18. Honesty is very important and this man who loves his partner confesses where he is weak and in need of making changes. He asks for forgiveness when he offends her and he does not hold back tears if they are sincere. (Jesus wept) He knows he has to be vulnerable even though he is a spiritual leader. He is determined not to lie and completely open and honest hoping for unconditional love and acceptance from her. They don't accept the wrong behavior toward each other but they love and accept each other unconditionally. This man seeks forgiveness and reconciliation in all areas to strengthen the relationship.

19. He goes to God for help all the time. He has complete dependence on God through daily prayer. Lord direct my steps to do your will and love my family and all people. Fill me with your Spirit and keep me from falling into temptation.

20. He keeps the relationship from boredom or too much familiarity. He keeps it fresh and creative and exciting. He makes his wife laugh and smile often and knows the right balance. He keeps the smiles coming and joy is in his house! Laughter is good medicine and there are daily doses for both of them.

21. When he makes physical love to her he concentrates on how he can give her pleasure. He is patient with foreplay and tender in his words. He reads the stages she is going through and his goal is to give her the sexual climax she would desire knowing it may take longer for her to reach it. He reads her right and respects her boundaries at all times. Agreement is the essence of the pleasure between them. He knows tenderness never pushes and he is not selfish or in a hurry. He lets her know what the Song of Songs in the bible really says in the Hebrew text!

22. He raises her to a higher level in knowledge by practicing the word of God. He does not just read in his bible and chew it. He gets on his feet and goes out to do it! He washes her with the water of the Word. He makes his bride more like Jesus. He is a counselor and a teacher. He is a helper and a preacher. He knows the Kingdom of

God consists of Righteousness, Peace, Joy, Power, and Love which is the greatest of all.

23. He is very quick to forgive and not easily angered. He knows the anger of man does not accomplish the righteousness of God. He absorbs all offenses against him. He tastes them and he does not swallow them. He chews them up and spits them out! He knows Jesus swallowed them all, digested them, died from them and rose again! He is calm and cool and Spirit controlled.

24. He takes up his cross and follows after Jesus. He goes the extra mile for his partner and even more when she is down and out or sick or troubled. He relies on the sensitivity of the Holy Spirit who governs his life. God is over him, through him, and in him! She gets the real deal from our wonderful Life Giver; the God who is Love!

There is no Door in which Tears do not pass with Grief or Joy

Our journey here on earth is filled with many doors that can lead to grief. There is only one door that can lead to everlasting joy. God has planted eternity in the human heart. (Ecclesiastes 3:11) NLT. The door of eternal life is in Jesus Christ. Ref. John 10:9 and Revelation 3:20-22. Open the door when Jesus knocks, and you will find the freedom to go in and out and discover what life is about! God gives us green pastures; the provision we are satisfied with. Many people can miss going in and out of the Jesus door. The parable in Luke 8:4-15 is called the parable of the sower. He can sow seeds in four different places.

1. The soil right next to the road.
2. The soil that is very rocky.
3. The soil where thorns are always growing.
4. The soil that is very good and produces much fruit.

Some people get to the edge of finding out about Jesus and never open the door or enter into the reality of God in Jesus Christ. I can assure you it is a reality! The birds ate the seed by the road and it got trampled. Some people miss the door Jesus has for them. Other people believe in the door Jesus has for them, but the foundation of their life has been very hard. They have hardness in their heart because of many bad experiences. They say they want Jesus and His door but the soil of their heart causes the seed of faith to wither. These are the ones who briefly entered the door and did not have the patience to persevere. In their self-pity, they withered away from faith with their rocky soil. Others go deeper into the door of Jesus and find more truth about God. They sowed their seed of faith in Him, but they have thorny soil. They have much of the world's mindset, and they are used to the pleasures of the world. While they say they believe and are seeking God, they are more concerned with the world's riches and pleasures. They are choking their faith to the point where they are not bearing the good fruit that Jesus called us to bear. Jesus wants fruit that will remain for eternity.

Faith in Christ does not carry a constant concern about riches and pleasure. This is the kind of person I want to focus on in this teaching. They miss the door of going in and out and finding what life is really about! The good soil of faith trusts in God with an eternal focus to serve Him and believe Him to meet every need we have. The good soil produces things that will last for eternity. The good soil people have character and attitudes that are in the Spirit of God with qualities that will never fade. The mindset of the good soil of faith is always an eternal perspective that keeps us living above a mindset on the things of this world. The world's mindset is very temporal, and it will fade away. The door that opens up to comfort and money often leads to many thorns in the soil and chokes the word of God out. It often leads to grief also. There are few exceptions where a rich man can handle stewardship of much wealth to the glory of God. It is hard for a rich man to enter the Kingdom of God. Jesus said this in Luke 18:24. The temporary doors of worldly comfort can be very deceptive. Deception is always where you don't see it clearly. When you can't recognize it is really happening, this defines deception. Some people who claim to be real Christians and have a very good portion of money will often reduce the Bible to an extracurricular influence in their life. The narrow road of discipleship involves rejection from unbelievers and suffering for doing what's right according to the scriptures. It is not a road to constant pleasure and constant enjoyment in the material things God has allowed us to have.

Those who want to live godly in Jesus Christ will be persecuted. (2 Timothy 3:12) If they persecuted me (Jesus) they will persecute you also. (John 15:20) Living for pleasure and entertainment alone and focused on the things of this world makes us an enemy of God. (James 4:4-5).

God wants to be much more than an extracurricular influence in the lives of people who have experienced new Life in Christ. Is He jealously desiring to be intimate and powerful through you? Examine your life and see if you can answer this question that has traveled through Christian faith circles. If you were arrested for being a Christian, and for your faith In Jesus, would your defense attorney be able to prove you are one? Or would the prosecuting attorney who has never lost a case, The Holy Spirit, win another one and convict you of falling short? Enjoy the good things in this world, and never make them your priority. The road that Jesus traveled has much more important things to be concerned with. He warns us that the love of money and the pleasures of this world can lead us astray and to grief. God's focus is for all people to spend eternity with Him. Refs. (John 6:40) (John 3:16) (John 14:6) (John 5:24) and many more.

Is God over you with His authority? Is God working through you? Is God in you? Is your friendship with the world one where you are making God known to them with His love? Are you doing good deeds and speaking the truth to them? Is the love sacrificial and sincere? Read Jeremiah 15:19. Are people turning to you because they see God in you?

That is God's purpose. As for you, the Christian, do not turn to them and join them in all they do when the mindset is only on the world. God can only work the good soil of your heart when you keep going in and out of the Jesus door, even when it gets difficult. This implies you have made your home with Him, and He has made his home with you. (John 14:23) There is one thing I believe is a good gauge to measure if you're coming to maturity as a Christian. Take the time to meditate on this next statement. A maturing Christian is when your bathtub full of tears from humility, honor, joy, and gratitude to God has more in it than your bathtub full of tears from grief! Keep going in and out with Jesus the Door, and you will surely see living with Him is much more! Amen!

Crucified with Christ and Raised to Glory!

Mr. Black, Mr. White, and Mr. Gray!

Introduction: In the Christian Life, some people think only black and white. But we should live in balance with both of them in sight.

Mr. Black, A brief description: pessimistic, negative, doubtful, critical, grumbling, low self-esteem, magnifies the problems in life, and has pity parties and inner strife!

Mr. Black focuses only on lack. He's under attack, and he might turn back. He's frustrated and forgetful of the power of the Cross. He doubts and complains, speaking only of loss. The irony is he can't see the Lord's gain because he's so often grumbling, and then he complains! Mr. Black, turn your eyes upon Jesus and off the world and its pain. He will heal your waywardness and fix what is lame. Grasp the right perspective and complete the story. You're not only crucified but raised to glory!

Advice and Encouragement: Mr. Black, God knows the end from the beginning, and remember, we win! You must have an eternal perspective and realize what we have been given in Christ. Set your mind on things above and not the things that are on earth. Colossians 3:2. NASB. Suffering on earth is momentary light affliction, as Paul writes to us from the Holy Spirit in 2nd Corinthians 4:17 (NASB).

The darkness in this life is increasing the joy of heaven for you, Mr. Black!

These are the identifying marks of Mr. Black: He lacks comprehension because he relies too much on feelings and external circumstances. He's led by his emotions and is not an objective thinker. He is living at a lower level of subjective immaturity. He demeans himself and is self-centered on his personal pain. Poor little me is his song in life. People don't like to be around him too much. Mr. Black is one of those guys that says, "I can't do it. I don't have the ability." He is fearful, lazy and could be called Mr. Ambivalent if he had an alias. He is often frozen with indecision, and he goes back and forth. He does not make an honest attempt to please God or people. He does not trust God for empowerment. He does not get used by God too often. He shows a false humility which is a form of pride. Are you a Mr. Black? Are you a Miss Black or a Mrs. Black?

Mr. White, A brief description: A perfectionist, not realistic, strict, without grace, has low self-esteem because he is not pleased with his performance. He walks around with a lot of self-inflicted bruises. He is demanding, and his standards are unreachable.

Mr. White says everything has to be right. But he gets disappointed, his goals out of sight. He claims victory to the point of no fight. He gets knocked off course, and experiences blight. He has failed to relate the day with the night only demanding joy and delight. He needs to look closer, see things as they are, and endure the darkness with the great morning star! (Jesus) Persevering in the darkness approving only of light, will make him much more effective as he enters the fight. In time he will see clearly and complete the story, crucified with Christ and raised to glory!

Advice and Encouragement: Mr. White, the body of sin is dying daily. We are not in our glorified bodies at this present time, even though it's as good as done from the Lord's perspective. As the Apostle Paul said in 1st Corinthians 13:12 NASB, now we see in a mirror dimly until the day we will know fully. Mr. White, you must accept, endure, absorb, and even devour the troubles, the pain, the mistakes, and the disappointments of this present time and whenever you can do something to make it better!

These are the identifying marks of Mr. White: Mr. White demands comprehension to the point where he moves out from under the authority of God. He does not have the submission in his heart to know his limitations as a fallen person in this world. He does not know when to let go of things he wants and trust God. He lacks a balanced understanding. He is looking for an equal correspondence with God regarding the evil that is happening. Job did the same thing. He never got an answer because evil does make sense and it is absent of the good logic God intends for us to have. Evil is a complete malfunction of all good reasoning, good purpose, and good order. It is devoid of God. Mr. White wants things perfect in a fallen world where sin is raging. He gets into a good works mode and loses the leading of the Holy Spirit, trying to keep the letter of the law to no avail. He is prideful, critical, legalistic, and self-righteous. He has trouble forgiving others and lacks the compassion, mercy, and grace of the Lord Jesus Christ.

Are you a Mr. White? Are you a Miss White or a Mrs. White?

Mr. Gray, A brief description: Positive, hopeful in attitude, a mature believer, a follower of Christ, and a leader to others. He is always realistic, practical, dynamic, and filled with the power of the Holy Spirit. He has the knowledge to fight darkness and walk in the light. He has a balanced walk of faith in Jesus Christ.

Mr. Gray has found the way. He adjusts the sails to what happens each day. With good times and bad times along his route, his perspective on both tells what life is about. He endures the evil in this fallen world and perseveres through the pain. He rejoices and hopes no matter what because he knows his faith's not in vain. He's grateful for the good times, and he recognizes them all. He knows his purpose never shunning his call. To be a light in the darkness and a life-giving flow, bringing grace and truth, saying it's Jesus, you must know! He remains steadfast in faith and completes the story. He has been crucified with Christ and raised to glory! + (Both Sides)

Advice and Encouragement: Mr. Gray, keep a balanced perspective and never become an either or thinker. It's good to grasp one thing and not let go of another. The man who fears God will avoid all extremes. Eccl.7:18 NIV. Be extreme in your love by obedience to God, and you will have balance in your life. Mr. Gray, you're getting brighter each day. You're trusting in Jesus to show you the way. You're enduring the darkness and saying yes to the light. You're overcoming the devil and winning the fight. Speak wisdom, love, and listen closely to all. Be steadfast in faith, always knowing your call! Remember the Cross, for it is always a plus. + There are two sides to the story when you walk with Jesus. These are the identifying marks of Mr. Gray: He sits at the feet of Jesus in solitude each day. He knows God's Word, and he often lives it out. He does not just sit around and chew it. He gets on his feet to go out and do it! He has joy and peace, and he greatly values all people. Red, Brown, Yellow, Black, and White, everyone is in his sight! He loves all of God's creation: the animals, birds, trees, flowers, mountains, clouds, the sky, the sun, the moon and the stars. If he stumbles and falls, he gets right back up and goes after God! He never quits or pushes too hard. He lives in the Now! He is God's witness to other people. He is making his love payments to other people because he knows he owes love to all. He can never repay God for the love he has received from the Lord. Ref. Romans 13:8. He is prepared to present the gospel message to all who ask him about his faith. He is prepared to build relationships with unbelievers hoping they will come to the appeal of Jesus Christ. He seizes each moment to bring glory to God. He seeks to comprehend life as God gives it to him, but he never demands comprehension. He trusts in God with his whole being. He loves the Lord, his God, with all his heart, soul, and mind.

Are you a Mr. Gray? Are you a Miss Gray or a Mrs. Gray?

Mr. Miss or Mrs. Gray, keep the Knowledge of the Cross in Perfect Balance!

The Cross is always a plus. It will always add to your life!

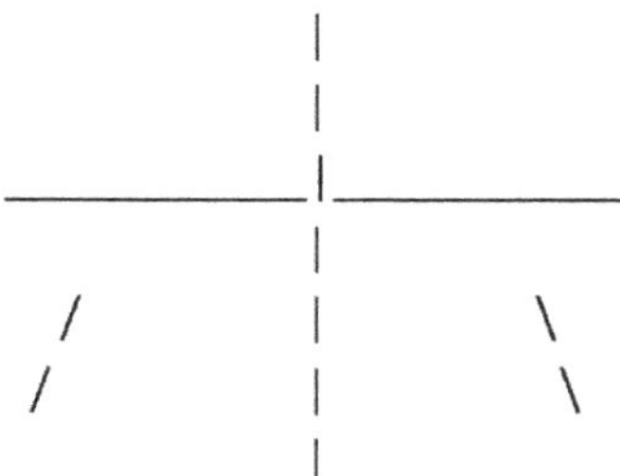

Mr. Black lives here. Not living the resurrection life God has given us! X	Mr. Gray lives here! A balanced walk with God! +	Mr. White lives here. Not living the crucified life God has called us to live! X

Mr. Miss or Mrs. Gray know they have been crucified with Christ and raised to glory! They are living a balanced life walking with God through Jesus Christ! They know the Cross is always a plus + and they have a steadfast walk with God!

SECTION THREE

Fine Divine Rhyme Time

The Wilderness is a place that is empty and barren. It's a place of waste and a place that's wild. It's a bewildering vastness and a perilous place. It's a place where it's hard to find direction. We can get lost and die in the wilderness!

Purpose: To WARN God's Children!

The Wilderness the Wilderness

The wilderness the wilderness is something we choose.
We don't like obeying; we often refuse.
We vie for it our way; we think we know best.
We deprive our own souls of God's peace loving rest.
The wilderness the wilderness is something we choose.
We say no to His authority and help ourselves lose.
With doubt in our mind and pride in our heart we hurt our relationship we push Him apart.
The wilderness the wilderness it hurts when we're there.
We will get bewildered and move toward despair.
But we must remember when we choose our own course the consequences of sin our Father will enforce.
The wilderness the wilderness it need not remain.
Just think of the price Jesus paid for our gain!
The wilderness the wilderness O Lord help us through.
Lord help us be faithful and obedient to you.
But to vie for control is not always bad.
If we vie for it God's Way we find we are glad!
The authority He has over us keeps us free in His grace.
And there's a crown of glory ending this marathon race!

Hands of Hope the Extension of God's Kindness!

Hands of Hope the Extension of God's kindness
Plus the power of God removing the blindness.
A feeding and a resurrection the intimacy and the power
Is what God's about and now is the hour!
Do the work of Evangelism it's not just words without deeds
The good news is transferred after meeting other people's needs.
Remember when you sow the seed of a good deed
You can deliver God's Word more effectively heard.
The word and the deeds of the cross are always a plus +
(God's Word +Good Deeds) The Trinity would say it's all about us!
Discover our functions and walk in our Love.
Bring others to heaven our plan from above.
Now is the time to respond to our call!
The Son went to the cross not for some but for all!
Hands of Hope and there's one other thing?
The feet that are moving and the Gospel they bring!

Overflow Should Always Go!

Overflow should always go; it's for giving back to those in lack.
Enough is enough God wants you full
With the abundant life He offers you.
But, it's not in good purpose if your overflow
Only stays in the bank so greed might grow.
Distribute in love to cover the lack
For the times other Christians are under attack.
Listen to God Mr. Overflow, if you really, sincerely want to grow!
Divide your food love your neighbor as self.
God wants equal shares regarding everyone's health.
When it came to his brothers, Barnabas sold all his land
He got a job after putting it all in God's hands.
He reached brothers in need and they started to see
God's love is designed by way of equality!
With wise discernment and ears that are tuned
With no partiality the Kingdom will bloom!
For the time could come when Mr. Overflow too
Finds himself in need of something generous and soon!
So keep it all moving to meet all the needs
Sowing into the kingdom planting eternal seeds!
For the righteous are judged they're accountable to God.
If you passed it around you'll get a well done nod.
But, if you kept more than enough thinking overflow is for you
You're missing God's heart that you really thought you knew!
God's not concerned with your riches on earth
If your heart has neglected other people who are hurt.
By way of equality, understand what this means
Bringing eternal value from all earthly things.
Share and divide keep some portions the same
And act like our God bringing glory to His Name!
(2 Cor. 8:9-15) (2 Cor. 9:6-11) (Isiah 58: 6-12) (Acts 4:36-37)

Lord Touch us again and again and again!

(More than one touch from God) Read Mark 8:22-25

Lord change our hearts make them ever true.
Help us see with eyes like you.
Red, Brown, Yellow, Black and White
People precious in your sight.
We want to see clearly please touch us again
So others can know you want to call them your friend.
If we see them as trees that can be walking about
We can see your connection to cause them to sprout.
You said you're the Vine that gives life to the branch
And the branch will grow up and go out where it's sent.
The touch of our salvation is only the start,
The process must reach into everyone's heart.
We must walk as trees that are filled with the vine
So the fruit that produced is the best one can find.
Lord touch us again and again and again
Until the likeness of Jesus is formed in all men!

Stop Climbing the Steps of the Crowded Ladder

To be famous in this world is not for us.
True fame and renown belong to Jesus!
Stop climbing the steps of the crowded ladder.
When it's all said and done the top will not matter.
There's a stairway to heaven that can only be reached
By trusting in Jesus and the gospel He preached.
Stop all your own climbing bow down at His feet.
Give thanks for His work eternal life is complete.
Getting caught in this world you never find real peace
So empty yourself and let Jesus increase! (John 3:30)
He gives us increase when we seek Him and pray.
He empowers our actions with love that will stay.
In a quiet place give God attention each day,
Then we accomplish His purpose and we don't go astray!

Mr. In and Out? Or Mr. Steadfast?

In and out a shout or a pout,
up and down a smile or a frown!
Back and forth an inconsistent sort,
on and off I rejoice or I scoff!
Quick and fast and I know I won't last,
if I get in a hurry I run out of gas!
Slothful and weak and my outcome looks bleak,
if I get caught in this world I'll never reach my peak!
I hit or I miss I have bliss or I quit
How can I deal with a man who's like this?
I come and I go and why I don't always know?
May God have mercy on my sorry soul!
And the last thing I know by His Spirit I was told;
I have one foot on each side at the fork in the road!
Who am I? I will ask will someone tell me at last.
I'm ready for death from the world and my past!
Now who will I become as God works in my task?
I'll be forever IN Christ and I'll be Mr. Steadfast!

1 Corinthians 15:58-NASB-Be Steadfast and immovable always abounding in the work of the Lord, knowing that your toil is not in vain in the Lord. Amen!

Why Should We Pray?

Why should we take the time to pray
when the world's full of trouble and so much comes our way?
Prayer puts our focus on God who gives breath to all men.
Through the troubles of this world we can be born again!
To connect with our God who brings peace when we call.
He's overcome all the trouble He wants salvation for all!
Pray Every Day!

Why should we take the time to pray when all the pain and suffering seems to be the display?
Jesus took all the pain prayer helps us follow His Way!
It's the pathway to glory toward the incorruptible day!
When all suffering and sorrow will be passed away.
Give thanks and give glory to Jesus the Way!
Pray Every Day!

Why should we take the time to pray when fear seems to be the order of the day?
Why should we pray when fear seems so huge?
Because God assures us in His Word He will be our refuge!
Prayer helps abide in the One who can save.
Worship Him thank Him give Him all the praise!
The spirit of fear is an invasion against you.
Recognize the battle for God will come through!
Prayer brings us the love that drives fear away.
It brings peace and courage to live life God's Way!
So let the prayer of faith bring love over fear.
It must not be absent it's what God wants to hear!
Pray Every Day!

Why should we take the time to pray when people are killing one another each day?
God gave His life with His Son's blood for their crime.
You can pray for salvation and this is the time!
God grieves for their crimes perhaps more than you do.
But He still loves the person the crime's coming through!

Separate sins from the sinner made in God's image too.
Praying for them is what real Christians do!
Pray every Day!

Why should we take the time to pray when we don't see any answers
or they're always delayed?
Because God's presence is enough He's the One who knows all!
And He knows the reason for what seems like a stall.
Until is the key word don't quit till you hear!
A moment of patience you must persevere.
Until is the key word don't quit till you hear!
Life on earth is so short and eternity is so near.
How long is your wait but a brief moment in time.
Compared to living forever in God's Glory Divine?
Pray Every Day!

The prayer bowls of heaven must get filled by the throne.
Our prayers are rising up to our eternal home.
The prayer bowls will tip and pour the best answer of all
Our Rapture to heaven in exchange for the fall!
Be patient and pray, persist in each day
Keep following Jesus or you could slip away!
Pray Every Day!

For the ones who don't pray who are absent each day
you're posing this question and here's what you say,
why should I get out of bed to pray when my body is in union with my mattress?
This is God's answer for you! Because it's better to pray than to lay and decay!
For those who don't pray stay in the bed of the dead! Rise Up! Says the Lord!
Start living instead! For when you pray you find true rest each day! You're coming to
know God and Living His Way!
PRAY EVERY DAY!

Me! Me! Me!—How Self-Centered can Me Be?

Sometimes it seems that all you see is people saying what about me?
Deep down inside self-centeredness lies and they're never ever satisfied.
Down in their hearts there's something screaming
they're searching for their purpose and meaning.
If only they would stop and think
Life is not working something stinks!
There's no contentment and no peace how can their struggle be released?
Look up oh finite man and see that heaven is calling out to thee!
For Jesus is the Lord of life He wants to remove your inner strife!
Why don't you turn to Him right now?
Just drop your pride and choose to bow!
Confess your wrongs and invite Him in He will enter your heart with a remedy for sin!
He poured out His blood so you could live
By His loving offer to forgive!
So what's your response for He's calling to thee
Now Jesus is asking! What about Me?

Mercy and Grace God's Mercy and Grace

The arms of Jesus were nailed wide apart
To show us the extent of His loving heart.
Mercy and Grace God's Mercy and Grace
The Son became sin He was punished in our place.
Our sins are forgiven they have all been erased.
The resurrection of Jesus to give us heavens place!
Mercy and Grace God's Mercy and Grace
There's no greater blessing that can take its place!
Rejoice and give thanks for God's mercy and grace.
Obey what He says and challenge others to face.
The love that is waiting for God wants to embrace
The people who cry for His Mercy and Grace!

Obedience is a Humble Affair!

God has never set a time for us to ever disobey.
We choose to sin we make that choice the malfunction of our own way.
He allows our disobedience but know He's never the cause!
If we would think about the consequence, it would be very wise to pause.
There's no room for pride no room anywhere.
We have all been called to a humble affair.
So bow before God the fear of the Lord present there!
And He will always keep you in His peace loving care!

Get off Your Lofty Pedestal

Get off your Lofty Pedestal with no steps to bring you higher.
You put yourself there by thinking you were someone to admire.
But now that you're there you will really find out it's not the place to be.
There's no steps to get down you can only fall and it leads to tragedy!
The proud will be humbled they may even die!
It depends on how long they keep their head in the sky!
All self-exaltation will come to a halt at the judgement of God the only One to exalt!

Walk and Talk the Gospel

(See Philippians 1:13-18)

I will walk it when I talk it, I will talk it when I stumble.
God always picks me right back up and makes the devil grumble.
I know it's best to abide in Christ, become as steady as I can
His Grace is given to His plan; He empowers what it demands.
His life is truly in me to work and choose His way.
He will not stop the process His life must be displayed!
I accept the yoke He offers, it's a constant walk each day.
He carries the heavy burdens He's the everlasting Way!
So, I walk it, talk it, make Him known; He gives the words to say.
Now! Is the time salvation waits, there should be no delay!
I talk it when I walk it, yes! Even when I stumble.
Humility is my rightful place, His Grace will make me humble.
How beautiful are the feet of those who bring GOOD NEWS! (The feet that are washed by Jesus and put into service.)
Are you saved? Are you covered by His cleansing blood?
Are your feet bringing the GOOD NEWS?
NOW! IS THE TIME FOR SALVATION!

EVANGEL ISM
Good news is salvation ministry.

EVANGEL IST
Good news it's salvation time.

Face to Face in Fellowship Gods with me Gods here!

There is nothing better than Face to Face
With open arms and sweet embrace!
It's what our God has made us for He knocks so gently we open the door.
We bow at His Presence we revel in awe our Master and Maker appears with no flaws!
Our hearts start to melt sanctification brings dross.
He gives us a bath in the blood of His Cross!

Transformed to His Image the Holy One works
Its death to the old man and all of his quirks!
Understanding is revealed and life's purpose comes clear
Because I opened the door and said Lord, Come in here!

The Eternal One's with me in the stillness we meet!
I stop all my scurry when I sit at his feet!
Remember this fact that removes all our fear,
when you really meet with God all hurry disappears!

Move in Faith and Walk in Love

Nothing ventured nothing gained we do it all in Jesus name.
Realize that standing still is not the way to do God's Will.
Seek His counsel hear His voice be careful when you make a choice.
Don't be anxious or start to race God will direct at the proper pace.
Move in Faith and Walk in Love as one who's truly born from above!

Sought--Brought---Bought---Preach---Teach---Keep!

When I was a vagrant and a wanderer, who moped and groped God sought me out!
When I was lost and alone and had no real home,
God chose me to be His very own!
God brought me out!
When I was lost in sin and had no peace within,
God paid the price there's redemption in Him!
God bought me out!
He sought me out, He brought me out, and He bought me out!
He preached me in, He will teach me in, and He will keep me in!
I thank God my Savior for eternal death could have been?
Now! I give Him my life because He took all my sin!

God's Way, not my way! Sing It!

Soon the time will come to enter through the veils torn curtain.
To face the Lord of Life and see His glory that's for certain.
I lived a life of lies until I found how much it hurt me.
But now I have been healed He gave me Gods Way!

Regrets all pass away no longer dwell on things that attacked me.
Mistakes I made in life, I've been set free from those that trapped me.
I live a life that's full I travel free on every highway,
Because I bowed to God no more with my way!

And there were times more than a few when I bit off more than I could chew
Because of pride and greed in me I felt so empty wanted to be free.
And then His love it came to me opened my eyes so I could see!
The truth was known my soul came home He gave me Gods Way!

God planned a life for me He redirected all my footsteps.
He had His hand on me He called me to obey His precepts.
He brought me through my grief and all the sadness life can give us.
He came to me in Jesus He gave me Gods Way!

For what is a man what has he got? If not the Lord then He has not.
To know the truth the love that's real. To come to God through Christ's appeal.
The record shows I came to know and live life Gods Way!
The record shows-- Christ took all the blows—
And gave me Gods way!
God's Way!

The Holy Spirit is the Real Mr. Clean! Sing It!

Mr. Clean gets rid of dirty things and sin from people in it.
Mr. Clean can change a person's life and bring them Jesus in it!
Mr. Clean, Holy Spirit, Mr. Clean!

Mr. Clean can show you Jesus how to walk with God each minute.
Mr. Clean reveals eternal life and all the blessings in it!
Mr. Clean, Holy Spirit, Mr. Clean!

Mr. Clean will use a sponge of truth absorbing and releasing.
Mr. Clean will rub the evil out and do for God what's pleasing!
Mr. Clean, Holy Spirit, Mr. Clean!

Mr. Clean will never stop working or let the sin continue.
Mr. Clean will never quit His job till He forms Jesus in you!
Mr. Clean, Holy Spirit, Mr. Clean! > Clean!! Clean!! Clean!!

(About the Author) Jim received a profound conversion experience to the call of Jesus Christ when He was saved. Jim studied Hermeneutics, Old and New Testament studies at Christian Life Bible College in Mount Prospect, Illinois.

Jim studied Theology, Counseling, and Ethics at Trinity Divinity School in Deerfield, Illinois. Jim learned much about a balanced view of life and scripture from his personal mentor, counselor, and Bible Scholar, Dr. Warren J Heard. Most importantly, Jim discovered the intimacy of God by becoming a strong advocate of solitude every morning and spends many hours alone with God. He has received a gift from God to be uniquely creative in communicating God's word. He revels in awe at the active presence of his truant officer, the Holy Spirit. He proclaims it is always a privilege and a pleasure to watch God work in people's lives. He knows he has a book with a broad range of teaching and a collection of insight and knowledge he could never have received by his own doing. He says his best times in life are every morning with his master and teacher for over 35 years and sharing it with all people. He is extremely grateful God has reconciled him through Jesus Christ and given him the privilege of being part of God's Kingdom. His main appeal is for all Christians to discover the depth of intimacy God wants with every one of His saved children. The finish line for our goal in the Christian life is the fullness of God's love that surpasses all knowledge. (Ephesians 3:19)

For more information contact us at info@advbooks.com

To purchase additional copies of this book, visit our bookstore at www.advbookstore.com

Orlando, Florida, USA
"*we bring dreams to life*"™
www.advbookstore.com

www.ingramcontent.com/pod-product-compliance
Lightning Source LLC
Chambersburg PA
CBHW071951090426
42740CB00011B/1894
* 9 7 8 1 5 9 7 5 5 7 2 2 1 *